CREATE A NEW LIFE
THROUGH THE

EYES
OF
YOUR

HEART

CREATE A NEW LIFE THROUGH THE

EYES

OF YOUR

HEART

FREDERIC DELARUE

Frederic Delarue Productions - Palm Springs, California – USA

Eyes of Your Heart: Create a New Life through the Eyes of Your Heart
© 2009 Frederic Delarue.

Cover Design by David Braucher (www.visiontovisual.com)
Interior Layout by Frederic Delarue
Cover Photos and Interior Illustrations © Frederic Delarue

Eyes of Your Heart: Create a New Life through the Eyes of Your Heart.
– First Edition

ISBN: 978-0-9824959-0-2
Library of Congress Control Number: 2009905344

Publisher Contact:

Frederic Delarue Productions
P.O. Box 799
Palm Springs, CA 92263-0799
U.S.A.

www.FredericDelarue.com

Printed in the United States of America

This book is dedicated:

To the Angels, the Archangels, the spirit guides, the Beings of Light, for looking after me, and for their continuous unconditional love;

To my paternal grand mother Yolande whom is watching over me from the luminous place where she is;

To my four legged Angel 'Tatane' who is with me in Spirit and who guided the design of the book cover;

To my parents whom always gave me the financial support needed in my childhood through adolescence to complete my musical studies and for giving me the freedom to live my own life;

To my closest friends for being an ongoing loving support;

To all of the friends and people I have met throughout life, whom were guided to be on my path for me to learn from the experiences encountered;

To all the elements of Nature that contributes daily to the balance of our planet earth: "Planet Earth, I love you, you are beautiful and I take the time to appreciate your extreme value and I do not take you for granted. I respect and honor you for being so generous and forgivable to what most of humans do with and of you."

I acknowledge and thank the Light that reigns and shines everywhere, even in the deepest obscurity of our own thoughts and in any event of our life.

About the Author

Frederic Delarue is a world-renowned music composer, inspirational author, spiritual teacher, motivational speaker, angel communicator, and currently resides in California.

Having had a Near Death Experience at age 12, becoming temporarily paralyzed at age 30, and later being visited by Jesus the day after a car accident at age 40, Frederic Delarue, a native of Chartres, France, has had many opportunities to see and experience the Blessings and the Light out of the tunnel.

His music is directly inspired by the Angels, soothes the body while uplifting the soul, relaxes, and focuses the mind on positive thoughts. His heartfelt music composed with a moving sincerity helps guide the listener by remembering to live the true radiance of their being.

He has also been blessed with the ability to play "The Music of Your Soul", a personalized CD that is created on demand based on the musical vibrations of someone's full name given to them at birth. Listening to your own vibrations helps to recollect and reconnect with the core essence of your being. It is an instant alignment while listening to the music of your soul.

Frederic was featured with Yanni, Kenny G, Vangelis and Kitaro on the benefit album, *Cousteau's Dream* in 2000 and has since composed, performed and produced the seven following albums of soothing music:
*Voyage of the Soul * Soaring with the Angels * Dolphins… A Message of Love * Symphony of Light * Reflection * A Mind Like an Ocean * Eyes of Your Heart*

For more information,
you can visit Frederic Delarue's website at:
www.FredericDelarue.com

CONTENTS

PROLOGUE

_____

For many years the Angels have asked me to write this book. It took a little while to accept and surrender to express in writing with words instead of with music notes. I am nicely surprised by the great Joy that the opportunity to write has given me. Words flew for three consecutive weeks like a beautiful improvisation of inspired angelic music. However, as I am not writing in my native language, I am asking for your understanding while reading this book. Know that I did my best, expressing words coming from my heart.

This book is the culmination of all the experiences encountered thus far in my life, and probably from my past lives as well.

I had wished to add some color photographs to illustrate some of the chapters but conscious that it would have brought up the cost of each book two to three times higher, I preferred to choose not to, in order to keep the cost affordably low for your convenience. However I highly invite you to view the photographs illustrating the chapters of this book at:

www.FredericDelarue.com/gallery.html
Click on **'Eyes of Your Heart Photographs'**

The book you are now holding in your hands has the vibration, the frequency, the sensibility to shift your consciousness by gently bringing forth your awareness to the different possibilities of perceiving an occurring event and allowing yourself to readjust the perception of an event that has already presented itself to you.

Life is a beautiful journey filled with beautiful moments and blessings that sometimes hide very well, in disguise. This book is about healing through the acceptance of what is, and what presents itself to you. When you believe that God created you in His image, it is therefore a perfect image that you are and reflect to the World. If we follow that statement, any imperfection would then be created by you, the ego and its folly.

The eyes of your heart however only see the beautiful perfection that you are today, without holding any judgments.

I invite you to read the pages of this book with an open and loving heart. Every written word comes from a heartfelt place and with a pure intention to help you to receive more clarity, discernment, and to offer you a different angle and perspective in the events of your life with a more positive attitude.

You are the co-creator of your own destiny, of your freedom, and not the victims of the events of your life, unless you chose to. You can choose to count your blessings or your misery.

I do not have the pretension to detain the total truth nor to impose anything on anyone therefore the opinions expressed are only the only result of my own experiences, which you may use to relate and identify that of your own.

This book is not just about me and my life. I offer you this beautiful and exhilarating intimate journey, using my own experiences in life as a support for you to find the clarity of your own truth and with the only purpose and intention of creating a luminous new life through opening the doors of awareness by seeing through the eyes of your own heart.

CHAPTER ONE

So Light in the Light

Ecrosnes, November 30, 1975. It was one of those winter afternoons in northern France when you get the sensation that the cold breeze is entering your entire body and freezing you, right down to the bone.

My parents were about to drive me to a healer, a few hours away from home, in regards to a small growth on my right foot that I had gotten from the swimming pool lessons at school. My father, Georges, was driving the car. My mother, Claudine, was in the passenger seat. My little brother, Fabrice, who was 5 at the time, was sitting in the back seat behind my dad, and myself, age 12, was behind my mom. My sister, Brigitte, was not part of this trip.

Chartres is a charming touristic town located fifteen minutes west of my parents' farm. It is world-renowned for its majestic gothic Cathedral, its sacred Labyrinth, and its pilgrimage. Chartres is my place of birth and as I also announce, my place of re-birth. It's as if I was born twice in 12 years time. You will understand this better after reading my experience in this chapter.

To go to the healer's home, we had to pass through the outskirts of Chartres by crossing a national road, equivalent to an interstate highway in the US. This road was feared by many as car accidents were common in that location. It was about 3 o'clock in the afternoon. The sun was extremely bright and low, which was making it difficult for anyone to see. The police were at the intersection to help people cross. I remember hearing the policeman tell my dad to go, but because he did not go right away, the policeman waved agitatedly to signal him to move faster. While crossing this national road, my eyes were suddenly captivated by a car, a Citroen DS that I could see from very far away, moving closer and closer so rapidly, that before I could even say anything, struck head-on at the door where I was sitting.

At that time in France, back seat belts were not required, so my brother and I did not have one. The extreme brutal shock of the collision ejected me a few feet above the car before my body crashed like a rock in the middle of the road. My parents' car, a Renault 16, was still spinning in a circle from the accident. Finally it stopped, by a miracle, at my right ear. My brother was thrown out of the car and, thanks to the flexibility of his youth, gently rolled onto a grass area on the side of the road which protected him from being hurt. My mom had some minor chest contusions due to the seat belt but she was OK. My dad was unhurt.

As for myself, my body was badly damaged. My face and ears were bleeding, and my left eye was out of its socket. I sustained many contusions and serious cranial fractures, leaving you to imagine the horrific vision for those who witnessed the scene.

However, for me, who experienced it with my heart and soul, it was one of the most beautiful, powerful, empowering and meaningful moments of my life. It taught me that there is definitely much more out there than what I could ever be able to see or experience with my eyes.

The day that changed my life had finally come. Lying in the middle of the road, I was in a deep coma. My body felt extremely heavy, yet I was feeling so light. Even though it may sound paradoxical, there is no other way to describe this feeling. Heavy, as my body felt like a mountain and I could not physically move or vocally respond, and light, because I was free to spiritually move out of my body, and fly anywhere I wished to, as if infinity was the limit. It was definitely an unusual yet magnificent experience.

Here is a way that can help you to understand this sensation. For those of you who may have had anesthesia before a surgery, do you recall when your body suddenly warms up a few seconds after the injection? As the anesthesia progresses through your body, you have the sensation that your head becomes heavier, and just between the moment when this is occurring and before you find yourself deeply asleep, your body and head feel extremely and densely heavy, so that you cannot move or vocally find the energy to respond anymore. This is that very moment that corresponds best to the description of how it felt to be in the deep coma. However, in the coma, you stay in that state until you either go further in the coma, having a Near Death

Experience (NDE), or until you come back to your living loved ones, on earth.

In this extra-sensitive state, I was able to hear everything, without being able to respond to anything. Every whisper, word, cry, and scream from anyone at the scene, felt amplified ten or twenty times, sometimes accompanied with echoes. I also could hear someone throwing up, and learned afterwards, that it was a woman whom had been behind our car and saw the accident as it happened. She was emotionally traumatized from seeing how high I was thrown out of the car before my body crashed onto the road. When I heard her, I wanted to give her a big comforting hug. I did not want her to be traumatized for me, because I was just fine where I was at. She was still being treated for emotional trauma after I left the hospital approximately three weeks later.

This paradox of heaviness and lightness was a present part of the moment I was experiencing that lasted many seconds, minutes and hours. This time allowed me to encounter this amazing, brilliant and unforgettable journey in the Light.

Most importantly, I was feeling wonderfully well. In contrast to that, hearing and feeling the pain, the sorrow, and the great suffering from all the people around me, including my parents and especially my dad, whom was very loud in despair, was almost unbearable. I remember very well that I could not understand why people were experiencing so much pain? For whom were they going through this emotional agony? Was it for me? How could it be for me? I was in the most beautiful place I could have ever imagined or could ever be. I was in Heaven! A place of light, of peace, of a love that cannot be found on earth, a love that is not human, a love that embraces you totally and unconditionally, a love that sets you free! Why would they feel this misery? I felt sorry for all of them, for that great suffering state they were in, because I was feeling the greatest. I was already in the highest vibrations and because they were not conscious of it, they were still living the misery of the lowest vibrations that is so common on earth.

I was so light in the Light. If only they could have been with me, I mean, if only they could have felt my feelings, my well-being, my heart, my soul, instead of focusing on the 'material' pain of the 'physical' me, they would have then felt my happiness and my peace in their hearts. I felt no pain whatsoever, and I wished they could have caressed that feeling of me soaring in that Light. However, a silence within would have been required for them to grasp that sensation, and they were unfortunately way too busy going through the torturing feelings of pain. In order for them to hear and/or feel me, they would have needed to be calm, serene, centered, grounded, in silence, to enter in contact with me this way. And this was very far away from the reality of their moment.

My mom knelt at my side and was softly talking to me. It felt good to hear her voice and to feel the loving presence of my mother, but I was unable to acknowledge her with words. I could only communicate mentally, by telepathy.

Different perceptions of the same moment, same scene; one of freedom, for me, and one of painful emotional attachment, for them!

My dad was crying and screaming, taking all the blame and guilt for doing this to his own son. Many other people were expressing their saddened feelings, for being emotionally moved by the vision of the bloody scene that my body was in.

I felt so much compassion for all of them. Let your imagination go for a moment and see yourself being in a peaceful, serene, soothing, comforting dreamy state, and then suddenly, have an angry crowd, screaming, yelling and crying, with the sounds being amplified ten to twenty times in your ears, into your head that had already suffered of contusions and fractures. Imagine how would you feel? Even a whisper yards away, could be heard very distinctly, as if it was next to your ears.

Those sounds containing the vibrations of agony were very heavy on me. If only they could have felt how I was feeling! I only wished they would have taken a moment to be with me, lovingly, purely and simply, instead of yelling and begging for my return. I was sending light to everyone to calm down their suffering and mentally talking to them, but everyone was too busy in their own experience of the pain to hear or feel me communicating in a way they were not even aware that could exist.

The deep coma I was in, leads me to demonstrate to all of you something that I find very essential. Of course, this was my own experience and I cannot speak for everyone who has been or is still in the coma at the time you are reading this. But I believe that if I experienced it, others may be in the same situation. I offer it to you as my perspective/perception of this incredible experience from someone who has lived through it.

In the deep coma, I was leaning towards the beautiful Light. On the other hand, I had people like my dad, who was begging me to come back to him, who was in need of having the 'physical' me back. He was crying, screaming, giving me the palette of suffering on earth. Let me ask you this question. "If you ever had the choice to decide between a beautiful Light of pure welcoming unconditional love, and the earthly human suffering, which one would you choose to go towards to?" The answer comes by itself. If you had to choose between a beautiful place where you feel embraced by a totally pure bright light with love, or a place where you feel the pain and suffering of people's neediness, the attachment of their emotions to the 'physical', as if you are only a body or nothing at all, what would you choose? You would choose the Light, of course!

Back at the scene, I then heard the sounds of the ambulance arriving. I was blessed to have the best nurse I could have ever got for the situation. After being transported into the ambulance, my dad came in, totally out of control, living in a state of constant folly where you do not even remember who you are, and what you are doing. Needless to say, it was not feeling good to hear as it was pushing me out of this world to go towards the garden of stars on the other side. I mentally communicated with the nurse, and told him to get my dad out of here, which he sensed right away. How fortunate I was to have had a nurse to understand the power of mental communication. Or was he a human angel on my path to protect me? He told my dad that I wanted him to leave the truck. My dad refused and aggressively responded (while crying) "Excuse me, I am his dad! So I can stay here. How can he ask something, he cannot talk? The accident is all because of me and I need to be with him." The 'human angel' had to be firm enough to ask him to step out. My dad felt so out of hand. It was sad for him, but at the same time, almost emotionless, I knew I needed to be alone, in the silence of my own Self, to live what is to follow. Again, try as much as you can to be aware that when you are in the Light, you do not have any more emotions of attachment. Those are simply earthly ties. Once we were both in the ambulance, the nurse whispered to me "Now you are OK. Don't worry. You can rest now". And it felt so good and so peaceful. The ambulance left the scene.

I remember that I could see myself from above. I could fly. I could not see any of the physical horrific details, as if the physical being was not the most important. I could fly. I was free and out of the body. This was pure Joy!

Suddenly, I slipped into another world. It felt like being inhaled into another dimension where silence was king. A world of silence! Floating, feet forward, going at fast pace in a totally dark tunnel shaped like a big tube, which would sometimes be slightly rounded and move upward. A bright light was at the end of that tunnel and I was going towards it. I was going faster and faster. I was coming closer and closer to this overwhelming beautiful loving Light. The Light was so bright, a little like the brightness you may experience on earth when your eyes are facing the sun. It felt as if this Light was opening its arms to welcome me with all its Love. It felt so good, so welcoming, so free, so peaceful, and so heavenly.

I was surrounded by 'Beings of Light', shaped like small kidney pools. They were everywhere, made of pure love. They all had various density and variations of white and gray. They looked like a substance made of cotton mixed with light. I was told that they are 'Beings of Light' and that they are everywhere around us, even on earth, at all times. They are part of our living system, they said. They are used as a gap between our negative emotions, and pure love. The Light became so close now and was so white and bright. It was a color and a brilliance that you would not be able to find on earth. I had never seen such a bright light before. It was so crisp and bright, yet it would not hurt any eye because it was made out of pure love. It was just magical, fairylike, hypnotic, enchanting and fascinating. I was admiring it, and overwhelmed with pure joy. It was calling me. I felt so light in the Light. I was experiencing the real unconditional love, and how more exciting could it be? Little did I know that it would become even more awe-inspiring, astonishing and empowering as the Angels magically appeared out of nowhere inside the tunnel, and said to me "You are okay. Everything is okay. We are with you. We love you". These words felt like a mother comforting her child with a rainstorm of pure unconditional love. What intrigued me, thinking about it, is that because I felt so small compared to the immensity of this tunnel, and because the Angels were so huge, so tall and big, the ratio of speed seemed different. While I felt like I was going so fast, the Angels did not seem to hardly move as they covered more space in the tunnel. It was amazing. It felt like floating while being transported in the Angels' heavenly arms.

The Light became so close that I finally entered into it.

The day that changed my life had finally come, and I will always cherish that moment with all my heart.

During this time, the ambulance arrived at the hospital, which found me between dimensions for a while; one where I was in the Light, and the other where I was able to hear people talking about me inside the hospital. I remember hearing distinctly the nurses yelling "Hurry up. Hurry up. It's serious here. He is dead, I think." I immediately flew outside the ambulance, looking below at the scene, and could see the nurses running towards the ambulance in a state of panic. It took no effort to fly. It happened the very instant I thought of doing it.

They took me inside the hospital while I was looking over the scene from above as we arrived in the emergency room. They prepared me briefly and injected me with something. I don't remember anything, until suddenly, the same way you wake up in the middle of the night before going back to your dream, I went back to my new world in the Light.

In this world of silence, I could feel and hear the vibrations of pure love and some delightful melodies, voices with such purity and clarity, like nothing we can hear on earth. Again, you can notice another paradox here where I talk of silence and hearing vibrations at the same time. This is what was so fascinating and so empowering to live. The lesson is, in order to hear clearly and purely, I had to be in a state of complete silence where I could finally find my Self. Here, no one was crying. Every Being knew that I was protected and loved, in the Light. It felt so good. Everything was on such a High Vibration. It is difficult to explain how I knew it was a high vibration, but I just knew it. It is like you just know it is, without having any doubt. It just is. That is what made it so peaceful, because every experience I caressed and felt, was so pure, and crystal clear. I was just breathing in the moment!

I was left alone for quite some time in my room at the hospital, floating above myself and was quite enjoying it. I felt so free, and so light with no boundaries, no limitations nor restrictions. It was a piece of Heaven. Next, I remembered that it was time to come back and that I had things to do on earth. It was time to get ready to come back. I suddenly felt like I was slowly re-entering, re-adjusting into my body, and the experience was not pleasant at all. Feeling the heaviness, the gravity of the body, which triggered to feel the pain all over again, was like living hell after Heaven. It felt so limiting, like being confined in a small cell in prison. It felt like freedom was over and I did not like it at all.

A nurse came to check me out, and screamed of excitement as if seeing me alive could have caused her a heart attack. She left the room while yelling "He is alive, he is alive. It's a miracle!" The surgeon came into the room accompanied by his assistant nurses and said "What do we have here. It is impossible he is alive." As if something went wrong for me to be alive. I could not talk yet but I could hear everything. I could feel his skeptical emotions about the reality I was for him. I could even see at times, even though everything seemed blurry. He did not seem to be very happy that I was alive. It may have disturbed his belief about death. Who knows! Then he talked to me, and I was able to start answering a little. He then left the room and I heard the nurses repeatedly saying that it was a miracle!

The surgeon did a wonderful job putting my left eye back in its socket. He later acknowledged to my parents that I was a total miracle, and the fact that I did not lose my eye was another miracle in itself. The eye popped out of its socket from the brutal force of the accident. Yet, a tiny filament was still attached to it and I remember him saying that it was impossible otherwise, that something or someone must have held that little tiny filament so they were able to fix it properly after putting in a few stitches. Without it, I would have lost my eye for good. I said, while smiling "Thank you, my Angels." I knew they held it so I would not lose my vision. It was such a powerful and overwhelming feeling. I stayed in the hospital for 3 weeks before I was released.

After I arrived home, every time I had to stand up or sit down, I would feel as if my head was spinning, which would make me feel dizzy. It was impossible to take any kind of elevator for many years afterwards. But I was home, alive, with my eyes seeing normally and I was on the mend.

This experience was one of the most beautiful moments of my life. It helped me to understand that I am never alone, and that there are many Angels out there, whose mission is to help me on earth. It also taught me that what I am able to see with my eyes is only about 10 to 15% of what is in this world. This day changed my life forever, as it has expanded the vision and the

11

perception of my life, and life in general. This is a good lesson for everyone.

Now I would like to share some personal insights about what I have learned from having had this NDE experience. Our perception of things, of life, of people, and the events we go through, can either have a negative affect or empower our lives. Every time we go through an event in our life, we are faced with making a choice, in terms of perceiving this event as bad or negative, or by choosing to see the positive side in every experience we have.

Because I chose to see the positive side of this event, this car accident has inspired my entire life and I will keep cherishing it with the grace that it deserves. It has taught me that no matter how tough episodes of our life may be, or may sound, we have the free will, the free choice to perceive them, as a victim or as a blessing in disguise. When you choose the latter, it changes your life forever and for the better as you allow yourself to accept the bigger picture of that event, even if it does not make any sense right away. The fact to accept it as truth, as Godly, will bring forth an outcome that is bigger than you can ever imagine. I call it blind faith. From that moment on, I blindly trust my intuitions and all that is happening in my life, as I know that, if they are happening to me, it is in the only goal to teach me something and empower me. If I believed in the bad, and in the negativity of events, then it would simply mean that I do not believe in God. When I use the word "God" throughout this book, I am referring to the Divine Source, The Universal Light, or whatever you choose to label it as.

My experience has also taught me a lot about death. We all know of someone whom we loved and who passed away. When that moment occurred in your life, how did you react? Did you find yourself crying? Crying for whom? Crying for them, or for losing the comfortable illusion of attachment, of you being able to touch them? There is a high probability that they were just fine, by reaching to the magnificent Kingdom of the Loving and Embracing Light. So, you may have simply ended up not crying for them after all, but to the illusion you had about the event or life itself. Life never ends. We are spiritual beings having a physical experience on Earth, and not the opposite way around. By acknowledging that, we never die as the soul never dies. The body may die, but the soul continues on its journey, and eventually if it chooses to, will explore a physical life in a different body later on.

After this near death experience, I was reborn at the age of 12, in a new me, for a new life. I will never be afraid of death as I have caressed it, as I have tasted its marvelous colors and flavors. Death is just a beautiful place where freedom and being limitless is king. I like to call it 'infinitude of expressions'.

Another immensurable blessing I invite you all to cherish every day of your life is to find a moment to stop your busy life, to stop running everywhere as if life was going to end in the next minute, and to trust and practice, as often as it may be, the power of silence.

It is only in the power of silence within, that you hear God, your inner voice, receive clarity on the many events you went through or you are currently going through, and may find who you truly are.

It is important to share with you, my personal insights about people in the coma and what to do, how to react, when you are faced with the situation in order to help to welcome the one in the deep coma, into your world.

While being in the deep coma, I would have loved to been talked to from the heart, very calmly, gently, softly, mentally, or a soft whisper and being shown the love that is awaiting me back on earth, surrounded by genuine human love. That would make me want to return to my loved ones on earth. Wouldn't you feel the same way? If people in the deep coma had to choose between the love in the Light, and the love on earth from people who can demonstrate to them sincerely that they love them unconditionally, and convince them of the abundance of love awaiting them on earth, I believe they would choose to come back in an instant. Only most people are unaware of this, and therefore, by expressing their raw, painful emotions of attachment, which triggers the vibrations and sounds of pain and suffering, they may unconsciously persuade the one in the coma to make the decision to go towards the Light.

Additionally, be open to the many different ways of communicating your love and thoughts to the ones you love and to the world. We have learned ways to communicate, in person or not, with our voice, with gesture, with writing, using the phone, and via e-mail. I would like you to consider other options, such as mental telepathy, that can be so important and the only way to communicate with those in the coma, or those experiencing a NDE or may I even dare to say, those who have already passed away to the radiance of the Light.

Love has no limits. Love has no boundaries. Love has no barriers. Love is infinite. Love can only be found in the mysterious and beautiful kingdom of infinitude, and this world can only be felt from within, from a calm and positive state of being. Illusion made out of selfishness and ownership is not part of this beautiful world of peace.

The beautiful soul that you are, who came to earth for a mission, and finds a home within a physical body, never dies. Your physical body dies as it is a temporary home to be able to experience life on earth, but your soul is always alive as it is eternally free.

CHAPTER TWO

SPIRITUAL SELF-DISCOVERY

After the NDE, which was the major episode of my life, there was not a day that passed without thinking of what had happened to me, what I saw, heard, felt, lived through, the Angels, the Beings of Light, the tunnel, the bright light, and the infinite amount of pure unconditional love.

I was in a constant mode of searching for the significance of the Light in my life, and why I had to experience it, and come back from it. What could I do with this knowledge and how could I share it? Was I the only one who has lived through this, or are there other people like me? I knew this had happened for a reason, as everything always seems to happen for a specific reason. I just did not know, yet.

In my family, I could not talk about it. Approaching the subject was considered taboo, and therefore was forbidden in the house. When I did start talking about it a few times, my dad would start crying, and blaming me for reminding him of what he did to me that day. He said it was like putting a knife on his body to remind him of his fault, his guiltiness. Of course, that was his perception, not mine. Nevertheless, this subject was prohibited.

I did not know who else to talk about it with. I was afraid that I might not be understood and I did not want to be judged. It became a spiritual journey of self discovery. I was being helped by the Angels and the elements of Nature, and it was on a long road ahead of me.

We were living in a small village located about 31 miles west of Paris and about 12 miles east of Chartres. My family was living on a farm belonging to the Delarue's for centuries. I was never really attracted to the cereal farm land. At the age of 4 and a half, I told my parents that I wanted to do music. They responded that it was not a career and that I was supposed to continue the family farm. I passionately insisted, which convinced them to let me try with a private piano teacher, Miss Madeleine Couturier, whose was living in a nearby town 3 miles away.

My dad used to perform in theatrical plays as a teenager, and by consequence traveled quite a bit throughout France. That's why I think he finally went into the core of his heart, remembered how he felt doing his artistic performances, and he accepted to let me have the privilege to get to experience that too.

Here is another major factor that may have contributed to the decision of my parents to let me do music. Both of my parents had a career that they had not chosen. My dad's dream was to be a baker and owning a store where he could display all of his artistic cakes by the window. However, his parents, even though they had 5 children, told him "No, you will be a farmer like all of your other sisters and brothers". At that time, it was still a common habit for the parents to impose upon their children to take over the profession that they had established, in order not to dishonor them. My mom's greatest wish was to be a hairdresser. Even though she was a unique child, her parents told her "No, you will be a farm girl".

As in most cases of abuse, it is known that the 'victim' keeps repeating and reproducing the same pattern over and over onto their children, which eventually will perpetuate it to each following generation as the cycle continues. So I am forever grateful to my parents for having the courage to cut off the ties to that painful tradition, or should I say curse, and let me do what I really wished to do, from all my heart, MUSIC! Even if they did not believe in it as a tangible career, they accepted to open the doors for me into that world, so I would not have to suffer what their parents imposed upon them and forced them to endure.

I remember a very amusing anecdote regarding the very first time I went to my music lesson. I was so shy that I did not want to leave my mom's dress, where I loved to hide behind. When the teacher took my hand and forced me in, it became a bit dramatic as I almost bit her hand. This is how I made my entry in the music world (smile). After that little incident, I was going every week in the town of Gallardon to follow the lessons. Miss Couturier told my parents that I had some great potential for the future, so that made them very pleased.

There were not many things to do in the village, besides helping at the farm, which was not my main focus. However, I always preferred to help my mom in the kitchen, making cakes, preparing meals, cleaning the kitchen after each meal, and vac-uuming every Saturday morning. At the farm, every day had its tasks. Something regular was that we always had to arrange so we eat meals together and at regular hours. A meal without a member of the family was just unthinkable for my parents. We also had very strict rules on how to eat, and to respect the bread, the famous French baguette. A meal without bread was also unimaginable. If I would display the piece of bread that was given to me on its back, my dad would, for example, yell and order me to place it back the way it should be, by respect of the bread, by respect of the wheat they grow at the farm, by respect of their profession. Even though this was nonsense to the child that I was, I listened carefully to avoid further drama.

At school, we used to exchange correspondence with other kids from another school located about an hour west, towards Normandy. We had one pen pal to write to, which was fun be-cause we knew that at the end of the year, we would have the opportunity to visit them, and for me, that was my only vacation out of the village.

One day, at about age 5, my school teacher asked all of us to say what we would like to do later as a profession. Most boys answered that they wanted to do construction like their daddy, a carpenter, a farmer, or a plumber. Most girls answered that they wanted to be a teacher, a nurse, or a mom. I said "I want to be a theatrical director, a pianist or a singer." Of course, that had made the entire classroom laugh out as loud as they could and I could see the eyes of the teacher popping out from surprise. Even though I probably did not know what theatrical director meant, it felt just about right to say that as it came out very natu-rally. It actually came out before I had time to think about it. I was often being judged by them, from one way or another. After that day, I felt a bit diminished. After all, what did I know about becoming a pianist or a singer? Was I just being arrogant or pretentious, which would deserve me the right to be laughed at?

I was simply learning how judgments, with its fear based limitations can cause emotional traumas to one individual, but I was on the other hand, learning to know who I was and to keep strong. Once again, do I choose to be a victim or to see this incident as a blessing in disguise?

I had a very solitude childhood as the kids at school often rejected me from being integrated in their circles of friends. They would say "Delarue, you are just different." They would call me names, such as 'Beethoven', or 'big legs', as I was tall for my age. The rejection from others had followed me throughout my life. But this was just another beautiful lesson for me to learn, accept and embrace. I could have chosen to perceive, or worse to judge it as a curse on me, but instead I chose the positive side of it and accepted my difference with grace as much as I could. I was different, so be it!

Now, I totally understand the reason why I kept hearing that I was different. It was not a curse, but another blessing in disguise that I had to embrace with all my heart. Being different was and is honoring the uniqueness of who I am, and embrace this God given gift with my heart and soul. If I were not different, I would not be where I am at today.

Even though I did not receive any specific religious education, apart from going to church to do my communion, I had this natural confidence that God loved me and supported me, no matter what. The sermons from the Catholic Priest would not resonate with me at all. It felt so false to my heart. But the God that loved and supported me unconditionally did and helped me through this day.

The fact that the other kids were rejecting me, forced me to be on my own most of the time, forced me to learn how to enjoy being on my own, which by consequence, forced me to focus, and naturally taught me what was essential in life. Through the power of silence and solitude, I quickly realized that I was never alone, as I had the company of the Angels, of the birds, the flowers, the butterflies, the animals in the fields such as the rabbits, cats, dogs, and I would talk to anything, any being, any flower, any living essence that was breathing. I was living deep Joy within as I was learning to communicate with beings that would never judge me.

In this case, this was another blessing in disguise to be rejected by the other kids. I see it as if God divinely guided those kids to reject me to force me to know more of who I am, and learn to see the truth through the power of Nature, and have clarity on things of life, in general, to make of me a stronger more grounded, yet respectful, spiritual being.

I chose once again to see the positive and I so invite you to do the same for each and every event that has occurred in your life, especially for those where you felt hurt, harmed, aggressed, abused, rejected, hated, humiliated, and so forth.

As I would not find any human being of my age to love me for whom I was, this is when the music and my piano took a new dimension in my life. I discussed earlier how nature and the power of silence had given me strength and how this helped me to keep grounded and focused, and my piano also had played a very important role in the recovery of my near death experience, and in my solitude.

At home, the only being that I found to express my feelings, was my piano. It rapidly became my friend, my confidant, my comfort, my peace and my healing. Each time I was feeling sad, lonely, in emotional pain, or occupied by any negative thoughts, I would sit on the pew of my piano, and start playing whatever was coming through my hands. It was not long before I realize that playing the piano this way, for at least 5 to 10 minutes, would set my heart and my mind free of any kind of negativity. Just like that! I would then feel happy, and light again. My piano became my emotional support, and helped me to let go and release negative tensions and emotions. Such an uplifting experience that would never leave me! I had found a true friend that would never judge or hurt me, and furthermore, that would heal me each time.

At the age of 7, I received the divine message of a big part of my life, without knowing it. I was watching TV while Julien Clerc, a French singer, was presenting his new single, 'La Californie' ('California' in English). As soon as I heard the name of that song, I felt crazy of joy, and I started to sing loud while dancing, jumping up and down to the ceiling. This song just exhilarated me at the highest of my entire being. I felt so happy, joyful and loved the sound of California. I had no idea where it was on a map, but it sounded great and that's all that mattered to me. I remember saying to myself each time I listened to that song "I will go live one day in California. I will live there." The vibration of that feeling sounded like my own truth to follow. I kept it in mind for many, many years.

Between the age of 12 and 14 years old, I had lunches every day of the week with Yolande, my dear grandmother from my father's side. I was going to school in Gallardon, and she was living just 5 minutes walking distance from the school. She had been a widowed woman for many years. She was a special lady and would always take the time to prepare some very special homemade food for my enchantment. She used to share our feelings about life. She was not a religious person. She said she did not believe in what was said at the church. It sounded too judgmental and false to her. But she believed in something obviously as she was a very good genuine soul. One day she gave me a book, called 'The Wheel of Life', which explains the full circle in the law of attraction.

One time, my grandmother told me something about people who complain all the time that would never leave my mind. She said to me to be cautious of all the people I would encounter and who would spend so much energy complaining and telling anyone they don't have enough money, etc. She was saying "If you find people who keep complaining, it's because they still can, they still have the energy to do it, they often do it for greed anyway, so they are usually OK. But it's the ones who cannot complain anymore, who need to be taken seriously and helped." She wanted to protect me. She was a very wise and spiritual lady.

My dad was also used by the Divine plan to teach me how to keep strong and focused through the lessons of life. The straight piano that my parents bought for me to rehearse at home was located in the dining room. I remember one day, he came back from the fields while I was allowing my hands to play whatever was coming through on the piano. He entered the dining room and said to me, while walking towards his office "Ah, it's not by tapping like that on the keyboard of your piano that you're going to be successful." As if he knew what I was supposed to do to be a good pianist. He seemed to enjoy saying things like that, as this type of incident occurred more than once. Those words coming from his mouth was hurting me each time deep in my stomach, but then, I would feel like God and the Angels were telling me "Don't pay attention to what he just said. He does not know what he is saying (meaning he does not even know he is hurting you that much and probably does it, perpetuating what his dad had done to him, so he just does not know better). Keep playing. You are doing the right thing, my son. I love you. You are loved." I would then feel better, like relieved, and would start playing again, happy and strong. What my dad does not know is that by acting like this with me, it made me stronger by believing even more in myself. Of course I could have chosen to be the victim once again, but it was natural for me to prefer to be the victor. He could not understand that my improvisations were divinely guided. Instead, he was judging and killing it with his sharp words and tone in his voice. My parents hated it when I was not rehearsing the Classical pieces that I was supposed to learn for the next music lesson. They thought it was throwing money out the window, if I was not doing what my piano teacher told me to do. The truth is that I never really enjoyed having to play in a way my teacher imposed me to. I was always thinking "How does she know this is the right way to do it? Is there only one way? How does she know how Chopin or Mozart wanted it?" I guess I was rebellious about what I was taught at any school actually. I was always thinking "How do they know this is the truth? Just because it is writing in a book does not make it true." This was not fun for me, as I enjoyed much better to improvise, and to play through the eyes of my heart.

What I learned in my spiritual self discovery was that instead of putting myself down, and simply giving my power away to those who were rejecting me, or judging me, I learned to see from the eyes of my heart, I learned to see the bigger picture of why such events had occurred in my life. I will give you, in another chapter of this book, some exercises, thoughts, and insights that may be helpful to you, so you can start allowing yourself to also see only the positive in your life, and how to do it.

It also taught me to see life events as many pieces of a puzzle that I gather. If I judge one of them, or one that I do not like for whatever reason, I may throw it away, to avoid facing the blessing. And because of it, will never be able to finish the puzzle. But if I hold them without judgments, those pieces may be able to fit together, to find their perfect place, with clarity, when the puzzle is made whole and complete.

CHAPTER THREE

AN UNCONDITIONAL FRIENDSHIP

When I was fourteen years old, I met an unconditional friend which became my best companion, my strength and my source of inspiration.

It is an unfortunate but common practice, at least in France, that every year before the great summer vacation, people drop off their pets, cats or dogs in the middle of a rural area, far from a road, to make sure they would be unable to find their way back home.

However, this time their selfishness helped me to gain a new unconditional friendship that I would not have otherwise had.

With my parents, we had daily habits and one of them was that we would always have breakfast, lunches and dinners together as eating was a sacred practice and the only time of the day when the entire family was gathered. My mom was always, and still is, in charge of choosing the meals of the day, taking care of a large vegetable garden, picking up the vegetables needed for the day, and preparing meals for the entire family.

One day during lunch, my dad, who had always been seriously involved in the City Hall of the village, from being the Mayor Pro-Tem for many years to becoming the Mayor, told us that someone found a lost dog in the fields and brought him to them. I suddenly felt an indescribable joy within, and I asked if I could go see him in the afternoon, which was accepted. I will never forget the afternoon when I took my bicycle and went to see the dog. I met with him and instantly we became friends. We recognized each other in the eyes of our hearts. It was a done deal! I came back to the farm, walking with the dog on a leash. I named him Stan, but his nickname quickly became "Tatane".

Needless to tell you how shocked and angrily surprised my parents were when they saw me with that dog. Even though they admitted he was very cute and looked like a small version of a lion, they instantly argued that it was not possible to keep him as it would take too much responsibility, and that, I was just being unconscious about it. I told them that if I would bring him back, he would eventually end up in a shelter, and if nobody picks him up in the following week, he would be put down and that we could not contribute to that.

Tatane was part of the family and honored the series of the 7s. Amazingly, I was born 7 years after my sister, my brother was born 7 years after me, and Tatane arrived in our life 7 years after the birth of my brother. It made perfect sense that it was the right choice to count him part of our family.

My dad refused to have the dog come inside of the house, so he attached him on a leash outside near the gate, and the dog barked all night long as he had to rebel for his freedom too. It took a very long time before Stan was totally accepted. I was so saddened that this new member of our family was treated like a 'dog' and not like a living being. I never understand why we human beings can do things to others that we would not want to have done to ourselves.

Tatane, as a puppy full of energy and aliveness would destroy anything he could find in the farm yard in the months that followed. Maybe he was just giving a hard time to the one who was not accepting him in the house (smile)?

I had two friends now, my piano and Tatane. One who was not judging or rejecting me, and one who was not laughing his ignorance back at me. One who loved me with his unconditional heart! We spent so many hours together, walking in the vast plains. We just enjoyed each other's company beyond words and this intimacy was empowering and uplifting to my heart and soul. Most of the time, he was reacting as if he knew how I was feeling or what I was thinking of. I was experiencing what true love means, for the very first time. The love attached to no condition. I communicated with him in a way that I did not know was possible. This alone, taught me a lot of the different ways of communication between beings and also taught me that we are all connected. We can all understand each other.

My relationship with Tatane was a true blessing. A blessing that I earned from accepting and honoring my difference from the other kids of the village instead of feeling like a martyr! I am forever grateful for experiencing with him the feeling of unconditional and infinite true love.

At home it was a different story. Tatane seemed to enjoy playing a totally different character than when he was with me. He would love to show his teeth to my dad while growling, just to show him that he can play the mean guy too. Of course, that alone would scare to death the 'patriarch' of the family.

I often noticed that most of the time, those who are so offended to have been treated unjustifiably, are the same people who blame, or sue others for not willing to see and accept what 'God' sent to them for their highest good, in order to learn and become a better person. The concept of what you send out, and what you get in return, is not yet totally understood by everyone. If all humans got that right, there would not be much hatred in this world.

After a few years, my parents eventually started to accept him, and cared for him as new member of the Delarue family. My dad, after the episode of rejecting him, reflecting his own fear of the unknown, started to realize that his new friend was following him everywhere, and was always so unconditionally happy each time he would see him. My dad started to feel loved by him, and eventually they became the best of friends. It is amusing to realize what fear based judgments can refrain and even block you from living and experiencing.

My dog, my Tatane, protected me, like an animal angel, till his death nine years later. He had an advanced intelligence. He knew my feelings and how to be a good friend. I thank God and the Angels for organizing our paths to cross.

People who drop their animals off in the wild enrage me, as it is often sad for the animal, but in this case, I would not have met him if he had not been released into the wild. From what could have been a sad experience for both of us (for him to be put down and for me not to have a living being as a true companion) emanated another blessing, the one for both of us to meet and become the greatest friends.

My four legged Angel friend will always be in my heart.

CHAPTER FOUR

THE WAKE UP CALL

At the age of 15, came time for me to choose a specialized College in relation to the career I wanted to do. My parents, who never truly believed that my life could be in the music field, thought that I should go study in Chartres, at a school specializing in accounting.

My piano teacher, however, another messenger in my life, was guided to convince my parents to orientate my life in a different direction. She knew of a school in the suburb of Paris, where music was taught in depth (analysis of Classical pieces, harmony, choir, etc) and wanted me to attend there. My parents were not thrilled with the idea of sending me to Paris and losing control over their son. My teacher knew how to reassure them by sharing her insight that she saw in my personality, someone who had a great potential in the music field.

Thanks to her divinely inspired help, I applied to the Experimental School of Music of Sèvres, in the western suburb of Paris. This school selected approximately about 11 students per year coming from all over France, making their selections based on a written musical test. Out of the hundreds of applicants, I placed 13th, just 2 spots shy from being accepted.

I was saddened by the fact that I had to apply to the accounting school instead, and have a job one day that I did not care for. However, another blessing arrived my way, as I received a phone call from the music school near Paris, saying that some students whom had won their entry cancelled, and by consequence, they were doing a second test to select a few more students and wanted to know if I was still interested. I begged my parents to give me another chance, which this time succeeded. I was so excited at the idea of moving to Paris and attending the only school of music of this kind in all of France. I was even more excited that my parents would accept to entirely fund my musical scholarship and lodging for four years.

Finally, I had an opportunity to make new friends and have a new start far away from home, and far away from the kids in the village. That's what I thought, but little did I know that life in Paris was a world apart from a farmer boy's life. Once again, I would find myself rejected from all the other boys and girls, because I was, you guessed it, 'different'. The main teacher of the school knew so well how to humiliate me in front of everyone by demonstrating how I was 'different'.

I remember a time when our main teacher tried to falsely gain our trust by asking us, in order to get to know us better, to write down on a piece of paper, with no reservations, the name of the singer, or the name of a composer that motivated us to enter that school, and to have a career in the music field. As an innocent soul, I wrote down the name of my favorite singer at the time. I loved her because she seemed so honest and true to herself, and she gave me the motivation to follow my passion. Her name is Mireille Mathieu. She was discovered during a TV show in 1965, an early version of 'American Idol' on French television. French people did not like her much as she kept a conservative look and was not modern enough for them. But, she did not care and I did not either. She was herself. I admired her heart, her joy, her passion, and her positive emotions when she was singing.

Apparently the teacher of the music school, that I prefer to not mention, had another opinion of her. She read loudly every single person's answer. When it came to mine, she chose to slowly articulate the name of the singer that I selected, which triggered everyone to laugh out loud at my answer. She looked at me with the arrogance of her ignorance, and said "Wow, he chose Mireille Mathieu. (*Accentuating very well on each syllable of her name*) Hmmm. well good luck to you. You have a long way to go. I am sure we are going to have fun together", before laughing out loud from her obvious unawareness.

This school was only teaching Classical music, and was not open at all to any other genres of music. My favorite composer was Claude Debussy as he was all about the emotion in each note played. I liked that. In order to graduate, we all had to pretend to speak the language the teachers imposed upon us. I rebelled many times internally thinking "How can they teach us how Bach or Mozart wanted their masterpieces played? Upon what are they basing their teaching?" I would go on and on. I was in a world where judgments and ignorance were brothers and sisters. A world with not much love, but a cynical falsely intellectual attitude! This is how I felt.

Luckily, I could resource, rejoice and embrace the beauty of life and unconditional love with Tatane during the weekends. I am forever filled with gratitude for his infinite heartfelt generosity and friendship.

The four years of rejection from the other students reminded me of the kids in the village. I was never invited to any of their crazy parties in the evenings. I had long conversations with God at that time, and would really feel that there was certainly a bigger picture, a greater reason why this was repeating in my life, so I forgave them mentally. I just did not know yet, why. More importantly, I had accepted it peacefully, not as a fatality but as a benediction.

Four years later, at the age of 19, I graduated and was given my first job in the Classical Music Department of the record label, Pathé Marconi-EMI France.
I was living with an elderly lady, renting a room at the top of her suburban house. I enjoyed the street that this home was on, as there were lots of trees, lots of nature, and the people were nice in that neighborhood. From my window, I enjoyed the successive seasons, from the flowers blossoming in the trees during springtime, the romantic warmth of the sunshine combined with the blue sky of the summer, the colorful leaves of the fall, and the snow in the winter, which was always so inspiring and uplifting to my soul.

Also at the age of 19, I stopped listening to classical music only and I started to open my horizons by listening to pop, easy listening, and dance, etc. I wanted to find my musical identity, so I started by composing a few songs, singing while creating music, and then began to combine original instrumental music with the sounds of nature. I still have this music on tapes today. I also enjoyed making what I called an audio-film clip. I would visualize a story in my mind, and put it into music and synchronized sounds. I had so much fun experimenting with it all.

Even though I was working and living in Paris, I was taking the train to go home every Friday right after work, as I started to give piano lessons to 20 students, ages 5 to 18 years old. That made my weekends busy from Friday evenings to Sunday mornings, non stop. I loved to teach them while inspiring them to give their best.

My dear piano teacher, Miss Couturier, used to organize an annual show in Gallardon at the end of every year where all of her students were able to showcase a nice piece of music that we had learned for the occasion. She would make us sing as well. I never forgot how much these annual shows motivated us all to give our best on stage. It was a moment of heaven for me. I was singing, playing the piano and I was on stage. I loved to be on stage. I was very shy in life, but as soon as I was on stage, my shyness disappeared. I felt like blossoming, breathing, and simply being alive. By the way, thanks to her as well, we went to Germany at the age of 11, just a year before my near death experience, to sing and play the piano through the Twin Cities Association between Gallardon, France and Amberg - Sulzbach-Rosenberg, Germany.

As Miss Couturier was not giving any more lessons at that time, I was renting her space to give the lessons, so it felt like I was continuing her work. She was so passionate about music and life, and she taught me a lot about how to perceive music and what was essential in music.

Most of the students were there, forced by their parents to learn the piano, because when they were children themselves, they did not have the opportunity to play as their parents would not allow it, nor had the funds to pay for lessons. Only a few of the children were there by their own will.

I liked to teach them as a foundation, that first of all, they had to establish, like they would do with any human being of their age they just met, a communication with the instrument, and a friendship. I also told them that it did not matter if they would never be very good at playing the piano, which took the awful pressure off of their shoulder and mind right away. I shared with them that there was an unlikely chance that they would become the new virtuoso in a Symphonic orchestra. Unlike the violins, an orchestra only needs one pianist. So they did not have to worry about that pressure either. Already, I had gained their trust, and they thought I was 'cool' for being so comforting to them and talking to them like a friend.

As I mentioned previously, parents were sending their children to fulfill their own never realized dream. Was it also the dream of their children? Of course not! Was I supposed to beat them up to force them to like to play the piano as well? You know the answer to that. What mattered to me, for them to understand, was that their new friend, the piano, was there to bring them comfort, pure love, serenity, inner peace, a certain type of affection, and healing as well.

I taught them that playing whatever was coming through their hands on their piano could be a way for them to release any type of stress or sadness through this form of artistic creativity. It is a bit like they were creating the music to heal their present stress or pain. When shared from their heart, to the Infinite Love of God, it released it in the ether. To feel that what is important is not how well they played the instrument, but how well they played in harmony with the dance of their heart. To learn to musically converse with the piano, and feel deep inside every single vibration, harmonic sound, and frequency radiating from each note that their hands were touching, and caressing. To feel the dance of sounds and to breathe out any feeling of sadness and inhale every healing sound their heart was actually producing through their hands and to practice being fully sensible of each moment. To release any negative emotions, spontaneously, just like that, is something that needs to be lived through in the entire being, to be fully understood. When one feels that, nothing in the world can ever bring you down, as you know what to do, and more importantly, how rewarding it feels to go back to a much higher place in your heart and soul.

It demonstrates to us all, how vital and consequential it is to be attentive to the blissful resonance of our heart.

I used the piano as an example as I am a pianist and was giving music lessons, but you can experience the same with any other musical instrument, or any other thing that brings the pure joy to your heart.

Some of my students were living in the midst of the storms of their parents divorcing, and they had no other outlet than to verbalize their feelings. They were so emotionally affected and saddened to see both parents that they loved so much, separate. This alone, was a huge motivation for me to teach them how to feel better each passing day with the help of their new friend, which at first they considered just as a 'material' musical instrument. What matters is the intention they sent out to the piano, so it can send them back the feeling of freedom. It's so simple. However, most of them had never thought the piano could have given them affection, comfort, and even instant healing. It was wonderful to see their happy smiling faces the following week, feel their excitement, and listen to them tell me that what I taught them, actually did work. They had discovered a gift of life that would follow them as long as they choose to remember.

They loved to come to their music lessons, because they said that I was 'different' (it sounds familiar) than any other teacher, just because I was respecting them, by simply taking the time to listen to them, to feel their feelings, and being cared for, was something they were all very grateful for.

I was also able to sense the true, natural artistic gifts of each child, which led to the writing, creation and production of four musical comedies. In one girl, I saw a singer. Laetitia had a terrible voice at the time and her mom thought I was just nuts to give so much attention to her singing. I told her to please trust me and give me a chance. With the permission to continue, we kept practicing. I told her not to judge her voice, and to only pay attention to the joy she could feel in her heart through singing. That was the key to unlock the magic. One Sunday morning, she received the revelation of her great gift. She was singing, and suddenly, she just hit the right note, and you should have seen the expression of the immediate radiance on her face. She knew that she just did it. Witnessing this moment is something I will treasure forever. This was the reason why I was teaching. Her voice was the most magnificent voice in the entire group. Her mother could not understand nor believe it. She thought I made a miracle of her, when actually all I did was to give her a positive attitude towards what was bringing so much joy in her heart. She had just manifested the deserved reward of her positive thoughts, of listening to her joyful heart, which created her new reality. When that moment occurred, we were both in awe, and she expressed the vivid need to give me a hug that meant all the words of the world.

Another kid was gifted for comedy. I felt it through the way of his natural expression. He had the ability to create jokes and make people laugh, but he was not aware of it and no one ever acknowledged that to him. The piano was not his thing. It was not bringing him joy. He was just there because his mom wanted him to be. It was like punishment to him. However, bringing him the awareness of his God given gift, and letting him express it a little each week, allowed him to accept to learn how to play the piano as well. He appreciated the fact that I was giving him something, and in return he was giving me the ease to teach him piano. It was a done deal.

The children all were so happy to come to our music lessons that some parents came to me, asking me what was going on, as if it was abnormal to see that their child was so thrilled about their music lessons. Sometimes, I wondered what their real motive was behind giving their children music lessons.

All this excitement of feeling ONE with the kids gave me the idea of creating an annual show with them. To produce a musical comedy combining all of their natural gifts, such as comedy, acting, singing, dancing, and piano demonstrations, etc.

This is how the writing, creation, and production of four musical comedies became very successful. I recall the great enthusiasm of the 500 people in the crowd for the first year. I also remember my mom coming at the intermission of that first show, saying to me that my dad sent her to say they were both impressed with me, my artistic work, and how I was able to bring people together like that. It was the first time they ever acknowledged anything like this towards me. Their praise and the success of the show was the reward of my trust in God, in the Angels, and in my heart.

Many years later, I met with some of my students and received the most beautiful heartfelt 'Award'. They shared that
they kept practicing what I taught them; releasing their tensions,
their negative emotions, by improvising, by letting their hands
play the song of their heart. The heart naturally knows the key
to unblock those emotions and to switch them into positive feelings. These testimonials could not have been more rewarding.

After these four years, came a time to take care of my own
career as a composer. I went to Paris and met with many different artistic directors and producers. I met with them gifted with
my natural innocence, as well as with a certain ignorance of their
world. I was far from foreseeing what would happen next. They
listened, and said while laughing at this music "What's that?
That's not what we're looking for. Do you really think this can
be a hit? Do you ever listen to the radio? My advice to you: Go
home. Listen to the radio and hear what's out there so you know
what we want, and then feel free to come back." Sure, I thought.
Should I already take a ticket for my next humiliation? It felt so
insulting and disrespectful to see them laughing at my creations,
which was 'my world'.

Of course, my ego was hurt but I was not aware of this at the
time. I did not know that this hurtful experience would bring
the best life lessons out of me. I did not realize it because I was
living it and feeling those raw emotions. I did not know what
the bigger picture was, yet.

This incident had set in motion the second major blessing in
disguise, as I took the decision to listen to the producers, to work
as hard as I could, to bring them what they wanted. I had
thought that after I sign a contract with them, I could slowly go
back to the unique creation of my true Self. My naïveté had cor-
nered me in the inferno of sharks.

I placed ads in magazines and found six singers whom dreamt of fame. For four years to be exact, I worked arduously to give them what they wanted to hear. A signed contract was the compensation expected. My friends at the time, whom were divinely guided to become my earthly messengers, and probably sent by the Angels, were warning me that this new 'pop music' that I was creating, was not me and that it was just OK, as I was trying to copy what was already professionally done by others. The uniqueness and magical touch of my heart could not be heard in these copycat creations. However it annoyed me to listen to them destroy my new illusionary motivation and like any human being with a free will, I made the choice to refuse their advices, which also altered some of my friendships with them. However, my determination was such that nothing could have ever stopped me. Well, that's what my ego thought. I believe that God loves us unconditionally and always gives us the comfort and support that we need, by guiding us, sending us emissaries, Angels or human messengers, to bring us back to our path in the event we let our 'Self' distracted from it. I was running away from the path of my true Self.

One day, a week before going on a leisure trip to Singapore, I started to feel sick. I went to the doctor and he diagnosed cysts growing on my colon. He wanted them removed before going to this tropical part of the world, to avoid any rapid out of control growth. He reassured me it was a minor surgery that only required a local anesthetic and that I would be home one hour later, so I said OK.

On the morning of the surgery, I had an odd feeling that pervaded my entire being attached to the outcome of the surgery. Should I cancel it? What should I do? It felt inappropriate to cancel with such short notice, so I went to the private hospital located in a town just east of Paris. Before the surgery, the nurse prepared me and injected the anesthesia shot into my lower back. The surgeon waited a little bit and then started to make an incision. I began shouting as I could feel the excruciating pain. He ordered the nurse to add some more liquid into my lower back. I could unmistakably sense the product being packed up somewhere, and it was not feeling right. I told the surgeon that it was hurting but his annoyed sigh made me think that he was not taking my request seriously. He was probably thinking I was just a wimp. He ordered the nurse to add more of that substance. And this little game continued until I told him that I really was not feeling well. He looked at me and said in a panic to his assistant while I was leaving my body "Merde, on est en train d' le perdre" ("F.ck, we're losing him.") His sudden fear made him add some other big words. I then lost consciousness.

When I woke up in the hospital, an unknown amount of hours later, I attempted to sit up and quickly realized that something was abnormal. I had no strength, so I touched my legs and realized that it felt like touching air. I touched my legs again and the same sensation occurred. It was like touching nothing. The physical legs that I could see with my eyes felt like air on the contact of my hands. I could not understand. I tried to move my toes, with no success. I touched my hip, and felt nothing. I immediately grasped that I was paralyzed. It was just like acknowledging it with no emotions attached. What had just happened so vividly, made perfect and whole sense to me, which allowed my acceptance to luminously envelope my entire body, heart, and soul.

With the loss of use and feeling of my legs, I felt the peace of God with the pure consciousness of surrender. The intense fear I felt previously had given way to a sacred sense of Divine Presence, a deep serenity, and complete freedom. It was a blissful acceptance and understanding. In order for me to explain this, I will need to backward a little bit in time.

A year after my near death experience, at the age of 13, I was watching a variety show on French television when the singer, Dalida, was on. I suddenly felt driven to play her name on my piano, by attributing a note to each letter, such as A for letter A, B for letter B, and so forth. Playing her name for about 7 minutes, I unexpectedly found myself seeing, as if peeking through a window that just opened like a multi dimensional part of the Universe, another Realm. I could clearly perceive her distress, her call for help, her true feelings, which were drastically different from the appearance we had of her on television. This shocked me vividly. It also scared me as I did not understand exactly what had happened. I did not know whether I caused this to occur, and if so, did I have the right to do it and see? What if I had violated a Universal Law, I wondered.

Without knowing it, I had experienced for the very first time, my main musical gift. I repeated the formula a few more times, with other celebrity names, and it would always instantly open up like a window of another dimension where the true feelings of that person could be perceived. It was fun and scary at the same time. The more I was practicing it, the quicker I would be able to perceive.

Lacking the opportunity to talk about it to anyone, I preferred to shut it off and refused it for many long years. There would not be a single day that passed by, without this haunting my thoughts. I was wondering: "Even if I had the right to do it, what use can I do with it, how could I ever help this singer from her distress?"
It felt worthless and was causing me a lot of stress. Eleven years later, when I was 24, the Medias announced the death of Dalida,

by committing suicide. This is the day when I understood a gift that I was able to perceive things, and it felt peaceful that I probably did not do anything wrong. I deeply knew, as my own truth, that one day would come, when I would have to face the fear based on this unknown world of perception of my gift. If it's a God given gift, how can I escape by not honoring it?

I had heard of some healers or mediums giving workshops and classes but again, I was cautious not to fall on some charlatans that do that for the sake of piling up the money. I knew of some of them who were misleading people, in the name of God, Jesus, the Angels, etc. So without knowing, I refused a little bit longer to develop my gift and tried as much as I could to avoid it. As the proverb says "You can run but you cannot hide", this is exactly what I did to myself for seventeen years. I tried to run away from my path, from fear based on the unknown, and something had to stop me.

When I woke up in the room of the private hospital, understanding that I was paralyzed, it made a total complete sense. I had been running away from my path, first, from my gift to create music based on someone's name, and second, running away from creating the soothing instrumental music, in order to please the French producers. Friends as messengers, tried to save me by warning me that they could not recognize me in this 'pop' music I was creating, but I chose to lose myself in it, by refusing to listen. In other words, nothing could stop me, unless God had some better ideas for me.

Being paralyzed was therefore the second huge Blessing in disguise of my life, as I could not escape anymore. I was face to face with the reality that I had co-created for my highest good. Instantly, I went into prayer and I said to God, the Angels, and to myself "Oh! God, I just got it. Oh! I am so sorry for being so stubborn and for not listening sooner. I could have done better, but I was afraid of everything. I ran away from what I am supposed to do. I promise you God, I promise you, the Angels, and I promise myself, that I will not be afraid anymore, and that I will be doing my life's work from now on, even if that means doing it from a wheelchair." This commitment was real. It was expressed with such sincerity that I felt some energy being released from the solar plexus area. I felt calm and serene.

A nurse came in and I told her the reason I became paralyzed. She was rude and told me "No you are not paralyzed. You are just waking up. Your body is still numb maybe, but it's going to come back. You are leaving soon anyway." I asked her "How could I leave soon, I cannot walk?" Then she said, while leaving the room that she would send the doctor to me. The surgeon arrived and totally denied the fact that I was paralyzed. They all deliberately chose not to pay attention to this fact. They knew that if they acknowledged an eventual mistake on their part that they could be sent to trial. So the best way was to continue denying it. They would rather consciously lie than deal with a lawsuit.

The day of my release had arrived. The doctors ignored the fact that I could not walk. But I just had to get out as they needed the room for somebody else. They released me with no word, not even a simple good bye from anyone. A friend of mine came to pick me up, and with much difficulty, finally succeeded to get me into his car and brought me to my apartment, located rue de Rochechouart, in the 9th district of Paris. My friend sat me on the couch and after a while, he left. Alone at home, I realized that I could not do anything. I tried to get a glass of water, as the kitchen was about 2 feet from the couch I was sitting on, and I fell. I started to sob and shed tears, as I understood that my dependent life was over, at least for now. I finally succeeded to crawl to the phone with the help of my arms and dialed the number of my parents. I did not know how to announce to them my news. When I heard the voice of my mom, no words could come out, only tears could be heard. My mom, not understanding why I was crying said "What's going on? Why are you crying? Tell me!" No words could flow. After a few minutes like that, my mom was stunned to hear me say, while sobbing "Mom, I am paralyzed." About two hours later, my brother and my dad were at my house and drove me to their home.

Even though I could not walk, the reality of life made me weep in despair. I was thinking of the job I loved so much. I was currently working for a dubbing company in the Champs Elysées. We would dub into French all the US soap operas, and series.

My parents called their family doctor the next morning. He was the same doctor I used to have since I was a child. He was a nice man whom always took the time to listen to his patients. They all comforted me a lot, with positive thoughts, saying that maybe I will be able to walk again with a good attitude. It felt good to hear that. However, my new reality was to accept being totally dependent of my family after enjoying being independent.

My friends and family tried to convince me to sue the doctors of the private hospital. But my major focus was to be able to walk again. I knew why this episode had occurred as I was the co-creator of it, but how could I ever reveal that to anyone, including my parents? I did not want to be judged. I decided not to pursue the idea of a lawsuit. Even if I did not appreciate the cowardly behavior of the doctors, I knew, most importantly, that God had certainly guided them to act upon the lesson I had to learn, which triggered to return to my path. I never believe in mistakes or coincidences because I know there is always a bigger picture than what we can see or feel at the time of an occurring event.

I had given my power away to the French Producers that convinced me to change my Self. And I was happy to be back to my true Self. Everything was so clear in my mind.

Every single day saw a little progress, from slowly feeling my toes, my legs, and then begin learning to stand up without falling. My lower back was so swollen from all that liquid they injected, which made it almost impossible to stand straight for a long time.

I finally finished my recovery by traveling to my favorite Greek island, Amorgos. I loved to travel to Greece. This would be my #1 destination as I loved the people and the experience there, especially in the less touristic islands. I wondered whether it was reasonable to plan for a recovery in Greece as I could not even walk perfectly yet. But my mom, with a genuine attitude, told me that she intuitively felt that because I loved Greece that much, it would bring my strength back, which did happen like she had foreseen it.

This episode taught me a lot about our judgments, why we sue, who we dare to blame, and so forth. Blaming or suing seems easier as it makes the other person the bad guy, instead of learning to be responsible. I believe in God, therefore, I cannot blame somebody else. It would then make me a victim that judges, and I do not think this feeling comes from a loving Godly nature. I also find amusing, the fact that in America, a nation that is so fundamentally based on Christian roots is also a nation that uses blame, judgments, wrong or right, and that practices lawsuits towards anyone so easily for the greed of money. It seems to me that there is a gap of misunderstanding somewhere.

I have learned through my own experiences that it is never too late to be aware of what we could have done better, and reverse, by going forward with more clarity and gratitude between ourselves.

CHAPTER FIVE

GREECE! OPA!

In Greek, Opa means partying and dancing. Greece! Ax! (Aaahhh – Imagine saying it like a Latin, with your arms raised towards the sky in a tone of ecstasy). "Ax!" represents well Greece in its splendor. It is hard to explain what Greece is, and who the Greek people are; you just have to live it! Greece, is the spontaneity of life, the traditions, the dramas, the sensuality, the passions, the colors, the smells, the food, the olive oil, the wine, the ouzo (typical anise drink), the retsina, the blue sky merging with the blue Mediterranean sea, the white, the green, the islands, the monasteries, the people, the hospitality, the generosity, the family, the Sacred, and the beaches… its all that make the scents of Joy in life! It is alive!

My Soul definitely has a strong connection to Greece and an affinity for its people. I could not imagine writing this book without spending some time demonstrating how this country makes me feel, and what it has taught me. I was born French, but I am probably feeling more Greek than French.

Each time I traveled to different countries, the locals thought I was either Italian, or German, and at last French, which I had always found very amusing. When I was still living in Paris, I was going to Greece one to three times a year. That should tell you how much I love it. Each time I was going there, locals thought I was part of them and spoke Greek to me, which motivated me to learn how to speak their beautiful language. They were always shocked to learn that I was French. I guess they thought I was Greek since I was simply feeling so comfortable there. It felt like my real home.

The Greek language resonates deep within me. It is so passionate, so fleshy, so alive, so spontaneous, so vivid, so colorful, so tasteful, and so dramatic. It is the Passion in all its pure excellence of expressions.

Traveling to this country of contrasts between the white and the blue, such is their national flag. I was naturally avoiding as much as I could, the big touristy destinations as you cannot taste the flavor of this Nation if you don't go meet the locals. This is another reason why I learned Greek so I could converse with the elderly locals and learn from them.

I loved the charm of Athens, its authentic farmers markets, its noises, its turbulence, the famous 'Plaka', which is the main tourist area at the foot of the world famous acropolis, Syntagma Square, with its Parliament , Monastiraki, with its typical subway with cats lying absolutely everywhere, Lycabettus Hill, from which you can enjoy a very romantic view at sunset, its tavernas, its food, its mountains, its churches, its typical narrow streets, its shops, its smells, its energy, its everything I should say.

I also enjoyed Thessaloniki, in the northern part of the country and its amazing surroundings. One of my favorite places was to go to Toroni; a beach located about 87 miles east of the city. It makes you think you are in the paradisiacal Seychelles Islands with crystal clear blue sea. Only the giant tortoises were missing.

However, my most favorite destination is the Cyclades Islands. Amorgos, Ax! I love to go to Amorgos! An island located between the touristic islands of Naxos in the north and Santorini in the south. Three main towns, one in the south, well frequented by the French, because the movie 'The Big Blue' was partly filmed there, Chora in the center, and Egiali, my favorite, in the northern part of the island and well frequented by the Germans. The view from the perched authentic village is astonishing. The ferry boat leaves you at the beach and then you have to walk up to the village or take a bus. The scents of nature, the olive groves, the colorful bougainvilleas, the blue and white painted cube houses, the typical blue domed churches, the white painted monastery of Panagia Hozoviotissa perched on a abrupt side of a cliff, the white painted windmills, and the white painted narrow roads within the village. Some of the local women still clothed in their typical dresses, men sitting while smoking and drinking at a taverna (Greek bistro), the music, the dance, the fishermen, and the aliveness of spirit of the people.

I am sure you had noticed that I have a special affection with this island (smile). Every time I have been to Greece, something wonderful has happened and made my entire vacation. Greece and the Netherlands are the two countries in Europe that I have been, where you can feel what hospitality means and I would like to share some beautiful, meaningful, and inspiring stories with you.

One day, I was overlooking the amazing scenery of the immense blue sea at sunset from the village of Egiali. It was a narrow road all painted in white and grey, with old homes on the left and on the right, you could admire the incredible spectacle of Nature. I found a place that I liked and stood there for quite some time, meditating in this peaceful setting. A house was behind me, and the front door was open. An elderly woman came out and slowly walked by my side, without a word. Her face was beautifully wrinkled by the Greek sun, and she wore very old clothes. She stood there next to me in silence for a few minutes, joining me to contemplate the idyllic evening. Sometimes I could feel she was looking at me and when I would look at her, she went back to look at the scenery. It was very cute, like a first romantic date when both play the shy birds. Then we started to talk in Greek a few words. She appreciated the fact that at my age (I was in my 20s) I was enjoying this astonishing view all alone. She asked me what I was doing in this village, as there was nothing for the youth, such as clubs, etc. I replied that it was exactly what wanted to live during my vacation; peace and quiet. I was being rejuvenated from the busy and draining Parisian life. This island was very peaceful as there were no cars. The only noises you could hear were donkeys in the distance in the surrounding hills. Then she left with a smile on her face, I looked at her and she waved to let me know to stay there longer.

After a few minutes, she came back with a present, an apple. She gave it to me with a knife and a small paper napkin. It found me speechless as I knew that locals did not have much money and therefore they had not much food to eat. It felt like she gave me all she had that evening, an apple and it was just for me, as she refused to share it. What made this scene so very special to my heart is that she had not cleaned this apple and a small ant was still running on it. Without that ant, it would not have been the same. It meant so much to me as I was imagining this apple sitting on her sink, where ants loved to walk in line next to the wall. It was an untouched moment, and she had given me a part of her daily life, a part of her, by not sweeping the apple of the ant or by not cleaning it. It came right from her kitchen, her home, her world, to my hand. And that made the whole story so special to me. I almost had tears in my eye. Telling the story and living it is so different. You had to feel the moment, the exchanged vibrations; it was powerfully beautiful with extreme kindness and of a great respect. It was magical. Before leaving, I asked her if I could take a picture of her, but she said no. Elderly Greek people do not like to have their face taken in pictures. I will always remember her, her smile, her softness, her extreme generosity and hospitality at heart. She is real and she has a special place in my heart, always. I am sure I will meet her again, when one day I go on to the other side of the Light.

I would like to share another story that took place in the same village. One evening, I went to an authentic taverna; a place where you only see the locals eating is usually a great sign of a promising delight for the taste-buds. I sat alone at a table outside, near the kitchen area, when several fishermen already sitting at a bigger table, asked me if I wanted to join them, which I did with great enthusiasm. They were so thrilled that I had accepted their invitation. They were eating the fishes they just had caught in the afternoon from the sea down below. This was, without any doubt, the freshest fish meal I ever had in my entire life. The taverna had typical folk Greek folk music and suddenly one of them stood up, started to sing loud and dance, and another fisherman did the same. Greeks are so spontaneous, and joyful. They enjoy life fully and it was always nice to witness. They made me try so many kinds of fish that I did not know. Some of them looked very odd. They were laughing. I believe my naiveté and my light spirit was making their day. They said to me that they were surprised that I trusted them to eat anything they were offering me, because most of the tourists they had offered their food to, refused to eat it. I enjoyed experimenting, especially when I felt it was coming from their hospitable genuine hearts. At one point, we had eaten everything that was available on the table. So we drank a bit more of some good white wine. One of the fishermen shouted to call the owner who was also the cook. She shouted back from the kitchen of the taverna, they spoke in Greek and then the fisherman went to the kitchen and came back to show me another big freshly caught fish. He asked me if I wanted to eat it. Everybody seemed very pleased. So she cooked it for us. The meal accompanied with ouzo and delicious white Greek wine was a memorable experience but most importantly, their company, and the fact they were happy to share with me the fish they had caught during the day. Everything was offered with joy and vitality, music and dance. It's the breath of life.

The most spiritual place in Amorgos was in the center of the island along the east coast. To get there at that time, you had to take an old bus that was driving along a dirt bumpy road on the edge of the cliffs bordering the islands of each side, to the town of Chora, which is a small authentic town, with very peaceful tavernas with great food and Greek coffee shops. From the center of town, you had to walk for about 30 minutes to the edge of the cliff. From there, you could already admire the monastery of Panagia Hozoviotissa, founded in 1088 and perched on the side of a cliff, 1,204 feet above sea level, overlooking a clear transparent blue sea where some people enjoyed bathing. You still had to walk up the cliff until reaching the narrow entrance of the monastery where many old pants of all sizes were waiting for you since you could not go inside wearing shorts. You had to bend to enter the monastery as the ceiling was so low and the steps were so narrow until you reach the first floor of the monastery. There a monk was waiting to serve a welcoming alcoholic beverage of their own concoction. That has been their tradition to offer this drink to any visitor for centuries. Then you continue walking to the second floor of the monastery where monks endlessly prayed. They were so kind. Every time I went to this very special place, I thought of staying there forever. It was a feeling of déjà vu, as if I was recalling another past life there. It felt so comforting, so welcoming, and so real. I could feel Peace and Wholeness. I was wondering how this place could have been in such a chaotic and rough environment. It felt almost like a giant man took the monastery in his hand and glued it against the abrupt cliff overlooking the blue transparent sea. It is just sensational and each time, it was heartbreaking to leave.

Another great story took place on the tiny island of Kouffonissia, between Naxos and Amorgos. The arrival of the big ferry boat to that tiny island was a dreamlike experience. It was close to dusk time and it felt very peaceful as the ferry arrived in the port through a small narrow and deep fjord. Thinking of this place, I can recall all the scents and sensations felt at that moment. These moments cannot leave your soul. They become a part of you. I was the only tourist to get off the ferry. Most of tourists prefer to go to Santorini, Naxos or Mykonos. I got off the boat alone, and while the ferry continued to its destination, I started to walk up the road to reach the only village of the island. The gentle sound of the light waves from the port plus the billions of sparkly stars above my head made it a dreamy, almost unreal moment of reverie. This small village had a small hotel held by villagers, a taverna and a few houses spread out here and there on the island. There were no cars, only donkeys. The experience was just exquisite. At the only taverna, the owner was cooking what was available for the day. You could choose the menu. It was either you like what I prepared today or you should like it anyway as there is nothing else. It was real Greek home cooking. The omelets for breakfast, the lunches and dinners were just delicious. The number of tourists on this island was inferior to the number of beaches. So we had about two isolated beaches for each of us and this made it a total and real paradise. All day at the beach, bathing in the pure crystal clear water where you can see your shadow down below while you swim and the noise of the day would come from a farmer passing by atop his donkey.

After a few days of total lazing about, I went to visit the small island of Heraklia, next to Kouffonissia and I walked for over 2 hours in the mountains to get to a peaceful fjord. Once at the fjord, I saw a couple of fishermen dressed with their typical black clothing on top of the mountain. They walked down the narrow rocky path of the mountain, atop their donkey. Arriving at the beach, they took their small fishing boat and went fishing a few hundred yards away. They threw their net in the sea and waited while talking to each other. What a different lifestyle they have when they take the time to breath, to talk, to share moments, and all they care about is having enough fresh food for the day, versus our busy life! A few minutes later, they got the net on the boat and came back to shore. I could not believe it when I saw that the net was filled with tiny fishes in such little time. I was the only tourist on that small beach as most tourists visiting this island would stay on the main beach near the port. The man talked to me in Greek and we conversed in a friendly manner. Then he asked me if I wanted some, showing me a large handful of fish. I was shocked and did not know how to respond. I was 2 hours away at least from the port of the island, so

I told them I would accept them with much gratitude but I did not know how to cook them. With a natural laid back Greek manner, he replied with a smile "Just make a fire here on the beach and cook them." It seemed so easy for him. They did not know they were talking to a Parisian who had no idea how to start a fire in the middle of nature (smile). So he said "Please take this fish" while giving me two or three handfuls of the tiny fishes that he placed into a bag. "Walk up the mountain and at about 30 minutes away you will see a taverna. Go there and Shout Yanni, that's the name of the owner and ask him to cook the fish for you. Half for you, half for him! OK?" I replied "Oh I saw that taverna on the way to here but it was closed." He said so naturally "Yeah of course, it is closed. He's probably napping. Just go there and yell his name, I am sure he will open and cook it for you." I could not believe such hospitality. They just gave their fish to a stranger they did not even know, just because they wanted to share a bit of their life with me. Wow! They also were so proud that a young French young man was making the effort to speak Greek with them, and that certainly influenced them as well for giving me the fish. I took a picture of him and his charming smiling lady, and asked them to write down their address on a piece of paper, so I can send them the picture by mail. They were so happy, honored and grateful. I walked up the fjord and arrived to the taverna. I yelled "Yanni", and after a while, a man came out and asked me what I wanted. I told him that I had just met the couple of fishermen and they asked me if you could cook half for me and keep the other half for you. "Ahh" he said, knowing who they were. Without any hesitation, he said "Of course, my friend. Just sit anywhere and I will be right back." The taverna was overlooking a 360 degrees blue Mediterranean Sea view. I sat at one of the tables on the terrace near a special wall with a window which gave the perspective to look through a live painting of the blue sea. It felt like being in the middle of a French Impressionist painting. From all around, you could admire the infinite blue sea. It was a special moment. The gentleman came with retsina, a Greek salad, some 'Greek' fries and the fried tiny fishes. It was a banquet of colors, of scents, of taste, of textures, of paradisiacal heaven on earth. He only asked me to pay for the salad and the drink. As the fish was to be shared in half, he did not charge me for his time and for opening the taverna just for me. Of course, I gave him a generous tip.

Moments like these make Greece my favorite destination in the world, where the locals are the most warm hearted and generous people I have ever met. Of course, to meet them, you need to dare to go beyond the typical tourist traps.

These people may appear to have nothing, yet they always find something to share, with a warm heart. They will all remain in my heart and my soul forever, and I will always cherish and share with others what they have done for me.

May God Bless them All, always. Opa!

CHAPTER SIX

THE SECRETS OF THE CLOUDS

The successive rejections that I had endured as a kid, and during College, had forced me to spend the majority of my time alone. That in itself, was a true Blessing because I was not distracted by anything or any other person, and it allowed me to stay grounded, focused, and most importantly, to remain myself.

I was spending a lot of time looking around me, observing nature, the sky, and the cloud formations and their movements, which I felt were always answering my questions. It also made me feel good as I felt connected to the Celestial and therefore to the Angels.

My mom always wondered what I was looking at in the sky. She thought I was in a dreamy state, looking at the sky for no reason. Instead of actively and physically working hard, like my parents have always done everyday of their life, I was in a dreamy state, looking at the clouds, and because of that, she expressed her concerns to others. No one around me could understand me, as no one ever took the time to ask me about my innermost feelings or what I had lived during my Near Death Experience, since it was considered a taboo subject at home.

The clouds have always been Sacred for me and very spiritual. They have been for a long time, my psychic friends. I formulate a question, and observe the clouds forming at that moment, and receive my answer, just like that, by trusting what I see, and any feeling that it triggers inside of me. Sometimes, it would take some imagination, but I rapidly understood that what I called imagination was real and revealed the truth. I was letting go and trusting the spirit of the clouds. The response would be as effective as when I trusted whatever came through my hands while playing the piano to release a negative thought, or to receive an answer to whatever was concerning me at that moment. Each answer from the sky manifested either by the shape of the clouds, their directions, their movements, their speed, their forms, their density, or their dance. They would be accompanied by a feeling that I had to learn to trust, and that feeling was my answer. When I was feeling down or lonely, I asked a question to God, to Jesus, to any Spirit from the Highest Realms, and I would look at the clouds, and watch them move and form and show me signs, which would intuitively trigger the meaning of the answer. For example, when I look at a cloud, it automatically makes me think of something I have seen before, like an image, a personage, a character, an animal, an object, which intuitively initiates the character of the answer. Now, knowing that we see, what we know is maybe 10-15% of what really is, just imagine how many things we may have in front of our eyes, only our brain does not recognize them, as we have not seen them before, or we were not aware they could look or feel like this.

When you start opening up your awareness to such possibilities, you may start seeing things you never noticed before. I had and still have a lot of joy doing that. We may see an angel shape on the mountain, because we have seen images of angels before, therefore we can recognize it. What if there were so many other signs on the mountain, in trees, in the sky, anywhere, that we could not recognize just because we have not seen them before, or was not part of our DNA program?

It has always been natural for me to communicate with the Higher Vibrations and Spirits of other Realms. With what I had lived through during my NDE at the age of 12, there was not a shadow of a doubt that many things existed, yet I could not see them with my eyes, simply because I did not know how to recognize them.

We, as human beings, seem to have a hard time with simplicity, such as finding the answers that sit right in front of us, or in our closest environment. Instead, we seem to find a certain enjoyment to complicate things by looking for answers outside of our world. The same applies when we try to find out where God is, as if He is somewhere in the distant sky, in the Universe, or whether He ever forgot about us, when He actually resides always within our Hearts.

Again remember that God has created us as His image, and therefore, we are as perfect as Him. He does not punish, he loves unconditionally. This is the God I believe in, not the one that others have tried to convince me to believe in so I can live in fear. I know better of myself and I hope you do too or that you will learn to do so, as well.

I like to take the time to observe my surroundings. I acknowledge that I live as a soul in physical form. I am a spiritual being living a physical experience, and not the other way around. By acknowledging this as my own truth, it helps me to be more responsible, more appreciative and grateful to the world we share and live in.

We share this planet with all the other beings and living forces. The animals, the insects, the mammals, the fishes, the plants, the flowers, the trees, the birds, the minerals, the rocks, the crystals, and so forth. We often forget that we live on a planet made of glaciers, mountains, hills, plains, deserts, dirt, sand, water, seas, oceans, rivers, streams, lakes, ponds, wind, rain, sun, vibrations. To all of them, we should not forget the 85-90% that we haven't yet learned to see with our physical eyes, such as the Angels, Archangels, Beings of Light, fairies, orbs, and even God, Jesus.

When you look at a strong tree, such as a sequoia, what do you feel? Imagine that you have the strength of a sequoia, grounded to the roots and elevated towards the celestial sky. You are the harmony and balance of the earth and sky. A strong wind would only caress you, because of your strength of knowing who you are. Nobody or nothing could ever disturb the powerful being that you are.

As long as you are in complete balance and harmony with your soul, your body, your Higher Self, your mind, your spirit, and your home during this lifetime (your body) will remain healthy.

Like a strong tree, learn to be and feel grounded to the roots of the earth and elevate your spirit to the celestial realm of the clouds and beyond.

Like the masculine and the feminine. Learn to be in perfect balance, harmony and peace, and stay in that frequency of well-being.

Look at the sky and the clouds and learn from what they are telling you.

Everything happens for a reason

Every IS for a reason

Be at peace!

CHAPTER SEVEN

DREAM YOUR LIFE, LIVE YOUR DREAMS

Being raised on a cereal farm, my dream had always been to live in Paris, then to live in America, and more specifically, in California. The song of the French singer, Julien Clerc 'La Californie' brought me so much Joy. I recall that when I heard it for the first at the age of 7, I was jumping up and down towards the ceiling from pure jollity and ecstasy within my heart and my soul. The resonance of the word 'California' was a real rapture for me.

After working for two months, I used that money to go to visit my friend, Lori, whom at the time, lived with her family near San Jose, California. I was so eager to see California with my eyes, and to feel it with my heart and my soul. I will never forget that first trip as it was heart and eye opening for me. When the plane first landed on the American soil at the San Francisco International Airport, I had tears of happiness. For the very first time in my life, it felt like this was more home than my home in France. Lori was so very nice to drive me everywhere from San Francisco, to Los Angeles, to San Diego, to Las Vegas, and I was just overwhelmed with exhilaration and lightheartedness. I did not want to leave, and therefore postponed my departure to France by one more week, staying in California for three weeks instead of the two I had originally planned. Lori has also always been very supportive of my music and always knew somehow that someday I would come to establish myself in the USA. One afternoon during that extra week, neighbors of her family invited us over. They had heard from Lori that I was a pianist and wanted me to play something for them. I remember this moment as if it happened yesterday. I played whatever came through me on their piano and the lady started to weep, saying that she had never heard such a beautiful and moving music and that it had touched her heart deeply. "It was as if Angels were playing", she even added. I thought she was just saying that to be polite towards my friend, Lori, and I chose not to believe it. Year after year, however, Lori, who was feeling the same thing as that lady, kept telling me over and over the same thing, wishing that I would take it seriously.

My last day in California had finally arrived, and at the moment the plane took off, I sobbed of sadness, of despair, my body was trembling and I felt sick in my stomach. It was as painful as if a young child was taken away from his mother. When the plane landed at the Paris International Airport, my parents could not understand my sad feelings and unfortunately took it personally. What I could not tell them was that I felt more at home in California than I ever felt in the country of my birth. I was already missing the range of colors reflecting on the mountains at various times of the day, especially the amazing pinkish, orange and reddish colors at sunset. I will never forget the first time I saw Lake Mead in Nevada at sunset, with the various scale of colors. It was amazing to me, just like a living a dream and I wished that dream to continue.

I had only felt at home in Greece and in America. Jean-Claude Secondé, the husband of Hélène Polesel-Secondé (whom had been my mentor for a year, guiding me to trust the messages of the Angels), did a painting of my aura and saw that this lifetime was the combination of two past lives; One in the Middle East where the mountains strangely resemble the ones in California, doing healing through massage, and the other as a devoted woman in a Greek monastery, playing music. That would totally explain my devotion to music, healing and spirituality in this current life. It also reminds me of when I was in my early 20's at an Acting School in Paris, our teacher was each time attributing me the roles of priests, or monks. He said that I was perfect for that role because it could have just been me. It made me smile as once again an outsider would instantly perceive and place me into the 'Spiritual' category.

A year later, I was back in California. This time, I went to Los Angeles and had an interview with a film production company. I gave them a cassette of my music, the same one that the French producers used to laugh at. They loved it so much that the producer gave me a script to compose the music of a movie about the Mount Everest. I had a great smile on my face flying back to Paris with the script in my hands. Unfortunately, six months later, I received a letter mentioning that the company had merged with another firm in New York City and that this project had been cancelled. However, what mattered most to me was that through this offer, they had given me the validation that I could have a career in California. At the same time, I was offered a job, thanks to my job at Emi France, at the Capitol Records Tower in Hollywood. I discussed it with my family and friends, but unfortunately none of them were ready to let me go and convinced me not to go.

Living in Paris was also a big dream of mine as a child. When I was 15 ½, I had moved to the suburb of Paris to follow my musical studies, and at 19 was enjoying the use of an apartment in the center of Paris that I had bought. I was so happy and proud of myself, to live in the City of Lights. However, after a few years, escaping to the countryside or the beaches felt more and more frequently needed during the weekends as I was rapidly disenchanted and my feeling about the city switched till it became a nightmare, a trap, and I soon got what I call the 'Parisian flu'; a contagious illness of being surrounded by people looking sad, angry, unhappy, aggressive, judgmental, busy, watching their watches at every breath, running always faster and faster, driving disrespectfully, honking with no patience, shouting, swearing, and so forth. By living with them, and having to breathe this flu, every time I had to take the subway (when everybody is thrown towards the physical of another), it became contagious to be just like everybody else. One thought remained in mind to resource: escaping for the weekend. Two days of freedom against five of imprisonment. A high price to pay to live in the most beautiful city in the world!

Without question, Paris is definitely a beautiful city of Lights, especially when you visit it at night when the magic of illuminations starts its daily show. It is truly a very beautiful and romantic city, with a lot of art galleries, culture, history, and incredible architecture. I was living near Montmartre, and enjoyed going almost every night for 15 years to the Sacred Heart Church where local artists make a living of their art, thanks to the tourists. I also enjoyed watching couples from all over the world waiting for the sunset overlooking the city from Montmartre to give each other a romantic kiss. This place was my resource as I was receiving a bowl of fresh air thanks to the exciting energy of the tourists.

One day, I was at an Embassy to apply for a Visa, when a gentleman from Quebec said to me, a very simple sentence that literally changed my life. He said "I don't understand why people are so aggressive and negative in this city. If they are not happy, they should change. But no, they are not happy, they complain every single day, they contaminate their entourage and they will do simply nothing to change it. I don't get this. If they are not happy with their life, why don't they do something about it? Why don't they change their life? Why don't they go live somewhere else?" He had come to Paris thinking that the grass was greener on the other side but like me, after a few years, realized that he did not want to suffer the Parisian negative energy and aggressiveness, and chose to move back to Canada. It strangely felt as if he had said this just for me and that day, I got it, accepted it, and knew from that moment on, that I could accomplish anything positive instead of complaining everyday like an illusionary victim.

He changed my life without knowing it. We live in a time of history where we can travel anywhere in the world. If I do not like my current reality, it is my responsibility to change it, and choose my new reality, to create a new life. It seems so simple. We are free beings. We can drive, fly, anywhere in the world to live wherever we want to, or almost anywhere. Conversely, we can also choose to be the victim of our own life. The question to ask ourselves is: Are we going to take responsibility and accountability for our actions?

From that moment on, my thoughts were constantly directed towards the goal to live in California, the goal that I had almost forgotten after refusing my first opportunity at the age of 20.

Eight months after the paralysis episode at the age of 30, I started to live my dreams, by following classes with a wonderful mentor, psychic and medium with the angels, Hélène Polesel-Secondé. She is one of the greatest souls, spirit and genuine people I had ever met. She is real and her integrity, impressive. I could not have found a better person to help me to trust my God given gifts, my intuitions and the messages from the angels. She told me that each psychic, medium and anyone with this ability, sees differently. Some see in color or in black and white, while others will see a movie passing by, or through symbols, signs, feelings that would trigger the answer, pictures, hearing voices, and so forth. It was very helpful to me as I was not aware of this. Before that, I thought that if I could not hear the voices like Hélène was hearing, I was not good enough. What a relief it was to know that there was no right or wrong way to do it, and that we all have our own way to feel things. The key is to trust the messages received.

Hélène also shared with me that the Angels said that I was being too much of a perfectionist in regards to my music, therefore judgmental towards it, which reflected consequently in never finishing anything as nothing would never be good enough for something to be worthy of being released, heard or read by anyone. She said to me that I needed to work on that.

The class lasted a few weekends throughout the year and I asked to apply for the second year. Her integrity is of such a high vibration that she refused to take my money. She said "Look Frederic, you need to apply and practice all that you learned here. Furthermore, you know probably more than I do anyway. If only you knew who you were." I told her "Cannot you tell me who I am?" She replied "Yes I could but it would not serve you to know it now. Everything happens for a reason, and in its due time. Keep practicing, and trusting your own intuitions. Keep your money as you will need it to go to the USA." I was stunned of such integrity and I am grateful to have been guided to learn through such a person.

Her husband, Jean-Claude Secondé, did an aura session with me. I was sitting in his office, in Paris, and he was behind me drawing my aura, from left to right, which meant from my past to my future. He told me many things about my life, and which past lives had a serious influence on this current lifetime. I did not know any of this before but as an open heart, thought it was very interesting. Whether you believe in these things or not, admit that what follows is quite intriguing. He said that the two lives that have a direct influence on my current life were lives of a loner; one where I was a man, a masseur in the Middle East, giving massages to people which allowed me, with the money earned, to continue my journey from Egypt to Libya, the other when I was a woman in a Greek monastery, and I was devoted to playing some kind of musical string instrument such as a sitar or something similar.

Interestingly enough, in this lifetime, the solitude felt during my childhood and adolescence reflected the lives of a loner and in regards to my music, many people say that it is a massage to their soul, so a combination of massage and music of spiritual realm as being a combination of a man and a woman, bringing harmony, earthly ground, devotion, healing and spirit of the two. I found his reading fascinating. I am forever grateful for being guided to meet them in this life.

I also met, almost at the same time, a French author, that taught me how to communicate with the trees and how to receive messages and healing from the trees. Marie Emilia Vannier has devoted her life to share her knowledge with others, to teach us how to be respectful of the living trees as there are also breathing and living beings on earth. Each time I see someone cutting a tree or a flower, I feel the pain of that living being. So more people like Marie Emilia are needed to bring awareness to people in the world that we live in a planet that breathes, that lives, and that we could choose to be more respectful towards the other beings who we share this planet with.

In the summer of 1998, while visiting a good friend of mine in the state of Washington, I also drove to visit for the first time the city of Vancouver, B.C., Canada, before heading to California, then flying back to Paris. This trip was very difficult as it appeared to test the solidity of my dreams.

When I first arrived in Vancouver, B.C., I felt like living within a dream. This city, to me, is one of the most beautiful, clean and magical cities in the world. The overall clean Downtown, the beaches of all kinds for everyone to enjoy freely what they like to do are kept voluntarily untouched. The forests, the colors of its various neighborhoods, the Stanley Park where so many people enjoy jogging or relaxing, some of the beaches near the University reminded me so much of French Riviera and Mallorca Island in Spain, and one of my favorite neighborhoods, Kitsilano Beach, where families enjoy their picnics and barbeques late at night on the immensity of this beach. Imagine a large breathtaking beach bordered by beautiful trees and the amazing color of this ocean, perceiving far away Bowen Island on your left, the northern coast in front of you, and the tall skyscraper buildings of the city with as majestic backdrop, its recognizable range of mountains, on your right. It is a very distinguished, impressive and enchanting panorama that you cannot forget. It felt like an inviting and desirable city to live in, which actually pondered in my mind. It felt like a high vibratory place on earth, which attracted me a lot.

I met with a film company and while the producer was smiling at the intensity of my indelible and enthusiastic attitude, he asked me to think it over and over again as, he brought to my awareness that the beautiful summer and weather I was enjoying so much, was not a realistic reflection of the daily life in this part of the world. However this city had done something to me. It also felt safe to be there, and the creative energy that emanates from this place is indescribably seducing.

Having Vancouver still vividly in my mind, the extreme haunting, dynamic, and vigorous energy of that city, the shock of arriving to L.A. was such that it provoked me to sob for almost two days, reevaluating my dream. A part of me wanted to move to Vancouver and the other remembered my soul mission to move to California, and more specifically to Southern California. Even though I loved San Francisco, I always felt that So. Cal. was home. It is a feeling within that you may also have sometimes when visiting places. Some feel homier, more connected to you than others, and it has nothing to do with the scenery or the beauty of the place, it is for a higher spiritual reason.

In Paris, I was working for a French television company, in the dubbing industry of American TV series, and films. My role was to mix the various sources of sounds for the French versions. I was also the only one at the time, to accept to work on the dubbed US soap operas by adding laughter after jokes, and coming from a different culture, this was not for everyone. But it was perfect for my light spirit. It is known that Americans laugh easily about anything, the opposite of French who are so reserved and serious. So my job was to dethrone that myth and make French people laugh (smile). Already, Hollywood and California was part of my life. When this company decided to lay off as many as 1000 people, I asked to be part of the plan, under condition to teach someone reliable to continue my work, which was accepted. I was laid off with a nice check, which I knew would help me for my new start, my new life in America.

At the time, I was renting a large house in the eastern suburb of Paris. One other important thing to mention is that when I was living in my apartment in Paris, I had many friends, but when I moved to this house slightly away from the city, friends forgot about Frederic. It is well known, as with anything in the world, that the laziness in us makes us miss opportunities that are outside the box. However I knew this was teaching and preparing me for something greater. It was too obvious to have no reason for it. A month after being laid off, the owner of the house, came to tell me that even though I was a remarkable tenant, he and his wife decided to sell this home. My heart illuminated of thousand sparkling bright stars, as I knew I was now free to live my dream.

One more step remained to pass, the one with my family. My mom told me that I had to go, that she did notice that I was never really totally happy in France and it was time for me to do what I always wanted to do, to follow my heart and even though it was heartbreaking for her to see her son move so far away she was supporting me. My entire family and friends all agreed.

I was free to start my new life.

CHAPTER EIGHT

THE TREASURE QUEST

The child I was, felt the joy with the song 'La Californie', the teenager I became was dreaming of my second life in one, and as a man I was finally living my dream.

I had been so eager to see California with my eyes and feel it with my heart and soul. I remembered buying books about this state when I was growing up, and what stunned me was that it said that all kinds of crazy people live in California, from elderly women wearing eccentric pink clothing, to all kinds of craziness in Venice Beach and this was exhilarating. It was my wish to see it with my own eyes. From a very traditional French life where fashion is a must, to a life where people do not care about what you wear or how you wear it seemed like a super heavenly state to live in. What I loved most was that people seemed to live the way they wanted to, without worrying about the opinions of others, which is totally opposite from life in most European countries.

My plane landed at the Los Angeles International Airport on September 19, 1999, Los Angeles, California. I came out of the airport carrying the 2 pieces of luggage that I had brought to start my new life. I knew absolutely no one on this new land. I rented a car and let myself be intuitively guided and stayed at the Best Western Sunset Plaza hotel on the Sunset Strip in West Hollywood for two nights. After that, I found a motel on Sunset Blvd that was offering special weekly prices, the Saharan Motor Hotel, where I stayed for many weeks. Driving down the streets of Santa Monica Blvd, Sunset Blvd, Beverly Hills, Santa Monica and Malibu beaches, and the windy road to Hollywood Lake and the famous Hollywood sign was just exhilarating. One of my first drives was to a city called Woodland Hills. Why Woodland Hills? Perhaps because the mountains of that area reminded me of cities in the middle of the desert! Only later I realized that the first car I had bought was from a Woodland Hills dealership and much later I even lived in that city.

After a vain attempt, I found an immigration attorney, whom I felt comfortable with to give my trust. The legal nightmare of the immigration formalities had started, which I endured daily for the following two years. The pressure of the requested papers, and all the things I was not allowed to do, was giving me so much stress that I would rather not go into detailing this topic. It was a high price to pay to be allowed to start a new life in the United States of America. If the Angels had shared with me how challenging and nerve racking it would have been on an emotion level, perhaps I would not have lived my dreams. It was that difficult.

In the meantime, I found a guest house to rent, in the Silverlake area, east of Los Angeles. I loved that one bedroom little home as you had to walk through an arch of bougainvilleas in order to get to the guest house. The owners were a very young couple, whom just had a baby girl. I stayed there over a year. I enjoyed the proximity of the beaches, the palm trees, the blue sky, the mild temperature, the flowers, the Jacarandas, hibiscus and bougainvilleas, and most importantly Griffith Park. I remember the first time I saw a Jacaranda tree in bloom. I had never seen a tree with blue flowers before. It felt like coming from another planet to me. What I loved the most though, living in proximity of busy Hollywood, is that I could find myself in the middle of the hilly countryside in just a few minutes. I was comparing it to Paris and thought that if I was living in Paris and wanted to see the same landscapes as the Hollywood Hills, I would have had to drive for at least 450 miles to find similar scenery.

I mentioned in a previous chapter about 'Sacred Heart Church' in Montmartre, Paris, where I used to live. I loved the romantic ambiance from the couples visiting from all over the world going here to get their paintings done before eating a typical French onion soup at one of the authentic restaurants at 'Place du Tertre' and kissing under the stars overlooking the entire city of Lights. Griffith Park was my new 'Sacred Heart' experience. This place gives me, each time, incredible and exceptional feelings. Vermont Blvd, from Hollywood Blvd going towards the hills, is bordered by very old oak trees and Spanish Tudors, and goes through the Park, where locals aim to barbeque, hike or play volleyball, etc. At the very top of the hill sits Griffith Observatory, majestically overlooking the entire City of Los Angeles and surroundings. Nothing can compare to the magic and astounding ambiance that takes place from sunset to dark. On clear days, you can see from East Los Angeles, downtown Los Angeles, all of Hollywood, West Hollywood, Beverly Hills, and out to the beaches of Santa Monica. It is the most breath-taking panorama I have ever seen of a city. Many like to go there to contemplate the colorful and romantic sunsets before dark. However, the real thrill starts at dusk, when your mind and spirit can bathe into the immensity of the animated sea of colored lights. Looking at the illuminated Vermont Blvd and Western Avenue from above gives you a sensation that these streets never end, that they merge into infinity. I have traveled a lot, but I must admit that this is one of the rare places on earth that provide me with such an inspiring uplifting feeling of freedom, as it provokes my entire being to virtually fly over the city, and this sensation is most exciting and empowering.

About a month after my new life, I met a wonderful person, to become a best friend, Juan-Carlos. We were both in the same situation with visas. The only difference is that he is from Peru. It felt good at least to know and have somebody to talk with. Los Angeles felt like such a free spirited Heaven to me as for the very first time in my life, I was able to meet people I could talk with about spirituality. I did not have to hide or be afraid to communicate about this subject anymore. It seemed like every person I was meeting was open to all types of healing modalities, western that we know, and eastern, as well as many other type of alternative methods.

After a year and a few months, I moved to Woodland Hills, which made me smile as this was one of the first places I had visited when I arrived to Los Angeles. I often enjoyed driving while letting Spirit guide me. I discovered many amazing places that not so many people know about by doing it that way.

A few weeks later, I was reassured by my immigration attorney that I would soon receive the official Visa 01. Many of the

French film directors I used to work with in Paris helped me by writing testimonials that were essential to receive such an honorable Visa. I was blessed to discern that all of the jobs I had in my life had their purpose in the acquisition of this Visa. However, I was not too amused by the fact that in order to receive it, I had to go back to France for an undetermined amount of time since it was up to the US Embassy. The next two months were the longest of my life. Once again, I was learning to be patient. A year later in 2002, I received my Green Card. This is also the time I started to panic, when I realized that all the money I had earned and saved from all my successive jobs in France, including my severance check, was almost gone. Effectively, I was living on spending money only since I was not authorized by the Immigration to do any kind of work activity until the reception of the Green Card.

It was then that the Angels announced to me that it was time for me to relocate. At the same moment when I asked them where, I received a feeling that I had to go to Tehachapi, California, with no more details. I remembered then when I used to visit California in my youth with my friend Lori, there was a site that always caught my attention more than the others. It was on Highway 58, going from Las Vegas to Bakersfield. As a passenger, I had the time to look at and appreciate the scenery, and at one particular place, something was always catching my attention. I was always wondering what that place was, and what was calling me there. It was on that Highway, after passing the town of Tehachapi, right after the exit to the small village of Caliente, Kern County, California. This moment would last like 3 seconds while driving by each and every time, and for all these years, I knew that something was calling me there. This time, I had to go see for myself. I called my friend, Juan-Carlos, and we both drove there. It is important to mention that I had no idea what I was going to do there, except that I had received the feeling to go visit that location after asking the Angels where I would be relocating. We took the windy road to Caliente, surrounded of comforting rolling hills, which made the scenery very picturesque bordered with cattle farms. Suddenly, before a turn in the road, I felt guided to ask Juan-Carlos to take a picture of the hill in front of us, which he did. At the time, I did not have a digital camera, so we could not see an immediate result of the pictures taken. After spending hours in that area, we drove back to Los Angeles. The big surprise came when I saw the developed photographs. One of them, particularly, had the face of a child upside down in the sky, approx. age 12. His eyes were precise and hypnotic, which was intriguing to say the least. I went to the place where I had the roll of film developed and asked a man working there if it could have been an error on their part, such as an imprint from another roll they had just developed prior to mine. But he said that it was impossible as this picture was in the middle of the roll and it was the only picture with a face of a child.

The question now became "Who is this boy and what is his message? Why would his Spirit appear in my picture? Was I supposed to help him? Was he missing?" All types of questions started to pop into my mind. I called a psychic that I knew back in Europe, and she told me that it was about relocating somewhere and that his eyes were telling me the direction I had to go. Another psychic from the Los Angeles area told me that it was, first of all, divinely guided, as his face appeared in the blue sky and that I was to focus on the opposite direction he is looking at, since his face was upside down.

I went back to the site and asked someone from the local newspaper if they knew of any child, or children missing in the area, approx. age 12, and if they would accept to publish this picture in their newspaper. I thought that maybe someone would recognize this child. She listened to me patiently and looked at the extraordinary picture, but at the end, said that they would not be able to help me more, as this paranormal topic would stir up controversy among locals and that it was not in the best interest for all involved. I thanked her for the time she spent listening to my story, and went back to the location where the picture had been taken, with detailed maps of the entire state and area. I wanted to know towards which city this kid was looking at, so I could draw a line and see where the opposite direction was. It appeared that he was looking towards Santa Barbara. Then I drew a line in the opposite direction from the perspective and angle I was in the Caliente hilly countryside and it gave me Palm Springs, which did not please me too much at the time. I came back home with this information.

A few weeks later, I received messages from the Angels within a dreamlike flash, or vision. There were successive words and images, such as a talkative tyrannosaurus, a cactus, a child climbing on top of a big rock, a dove, the word Indian, and the word wells. This was a new enigma to resolve. On my way to Palm Springs, I suddenly had a vision on my left of a tyranno-saurus with his mouth wide open, which stunned me. It was exactly the same as in the vision received previously. I then ar-rived in Palm Springs and stopped at the visitor center. There were many brochures and pictures and I became speechless when I saw a pamphlet with the picture of the kid climbing and reaching the top of a huge rock. I realized that the word Indian was largely used here as there are Indian reservations all around and there was even a city called Indian Wells. Wells was also a common word locally for the many hot springs in the area. Cac-tus symbolizing the desert area, it all made sense, or almost, as I still had the dove to figure out. I took a phone book and literally read all the pages to see where I could find a street named 'Dove'. It appeared that there was one in Indian Wells, in a gated community so I could not go check it out. Even though this enigma was not yet resolved, it made total sense that the successive angelic messages received, from the picture with the child's face upside down, to the ones described above, invited me to relocate to Palm Springs.

I see the steps in my life a bit like a treasure quest. I am told to go one place, which when followed with a blind Faith, tells me where to go next, and so forth.

It is quite a thrill to blindly trust Spirit!

CHAPTER NINE

PALM SPRINGS

My arrival to the Palm Springs area in March 2002 was so divinely orchestrated by the Angels and God. More things have happened here in the last ten years than in my first 35 years. Many doors opened all at once. Therefore, I will be mentioning in this chapter many of the events in the order they have occurred, but I will be detailing them in the chapters to follow.

I looked for a rental in Palm Springs, and the fact it was much cheaper than in the L.A. area was so appreciated at that time, as living in California for 2 years without being able to work had gulped down all of my savings. Each time I visited the Palm Springs area, I was always attracted to the city on the left of Interstate 10. It was an inexplicable natural magnetic attraction.

However, I tried to find rentals in the lower part of the Coachella Valley, from Palm Springs to Palm Desert, but it would never work out as someone would always rent the place I had chosen just before me. I took it as a sign it was not meant to be, but it became a frustration as well. A good friend of mine told me "Look, you feel attracted to go to that city, so go. After all, who cares what people are telling you not to do, and go wherever your heart tells you to go. Go back to that place that is calling you and you will know!" What a lesson! Juan-Carlos has always been such a good intuitive friend to me. Right away, my heart felt light again and the next morning, I was on the road to the desert. I followed my intuition, and arrived to a kiosk where I took a newspaper with some rental ads. I called one that had the description of what I was looking for, and went to see for myself. It was at 'Hidden Springs Golf Course Country Club', and it sounded wonderful. The manager showed me a nice remodeled mobile home, which I liked, then told me that there was another one to choose from. The smell, when I entered the second little home, was not pleasant at all, but for some reason, something was telling me that this was to be my home. She showed me the living room area and the patio, but when I saw the astonishing view of the golf course, the pond, the palm trees, with the backdrop of the San Jacinto and San Gorgonio Mountains, and the windmills, I knew I had found my house, and the house had found me. It was a happy marriage. The joy felt in my heart was confirming this was the right choice. I was like internally jumping up and down from exhilaration, the same feeling I had experienced when the 7 year old child that I was a long time ago, heard for the first time the word, 'California'.

I moved to this small mobile home with a million dollar view and with much happiness in my heart. The scenery from this home was so enchanting and inspiring. The golf course with the palm trees around the pond made you believe it was a natural oasis with the ducks, and the roadrunners. The mountains of San Jacinto and San Gorgonio, and the hills of Desert Hot Springs turned golden and reddish at sunset, and the windmills made it an absolute paradise on earth. The great sensation that the warmth of the desert and the abundant sunshine provided to my skin, my mood and all the aspects of my Being, is immensurable. I loved this feeling as if your body was surrounded by large hair dryers projecting the hottest air you can imagine. I personally adore feeling the warmth of that hot air on my body as it is a huge contrast with the cold humid air of Northern France.

I had a special affinity with the roadrunners which make me think of a story I cannot wait to narrate to you as it is so precious to me. Many times, the roadrunners came so close to me when I was getting a dose of natural vitamins, lying in the sun on my patio. One day, one of them entered my home, walked a few steps till reaching the area of my keyboards then gently left. It made me feel good to know that they felt as comfortable around me as I was around them. The camaraderie was so special between me and the roadrunners. Something very odd occurred a few days before I moved from there at the end of July 2005. The bay window to the patio was closed. A roadrunner came right at the bay window. I approached, and opened it a little, as I thought that perhaps he wanted to come in. He then looked at me right in the eye, which at first shocked me. I wish this scene could have been videotaped. He was making sounds that I never heard from a roadrunner before. I was used to the sounds they made when they came close to the house, but this time it was much different as it sounded almost human. He then started to bend his head and neck to his feet while making those very cute sounds, like reverences while singing or saying a poem. He did that for almost 20 minutes. I must tell you that facing a roadrunner for twenty minutes while doing reverences to me, is something I will not forget easily. It was very sweet, very gentle, very loving, and very special. Then he looked at me right in the eye again, and was speaking loudly. I was talking to him in a Frenchy English kind of mixture and my responsiveness triggered him to respond and talk more. It felt as if he knew I was leaving and was asking me why am I leaving them so soon? It also felt like an abundance of gratitude. Then he left, stopped, looked back, and ran away onto the golf course. I just could not believe that this roadrunner came to say good-bye and it almost made me want to stay there longer. I was moved to tears.

Also, on May 27, 2004, a neighbor who was practicing his golf techniques, shouted for me to come outside. A white dove was there in my garden. He walked on the patio before going on the side of my home over to where the car was parked, and then left. That was a very special birthday present from the Angels. They always find something very unusual and beautiful each year to celebrate that day with me and to remind me of their presence.

A few weeks after moving into my new home, a friend of mine came to visit me from Orange County, California, who had the thought of buying vacant land in the hills of Desert Hot Springs. We drove all over until he found a place he liked. We went there several times during the next few weeks, however each time I was to drive him to that lot I kept taking the wrong road again, and again, and again. I did not know why I was repeating the same 'mistake' each time. It was unusual for me to get lost, which intrigued me. Furthermore, mistakes are not part of my world as I know everything happens for a reason. One day, I decided to consciously make the same 'mistake' with full awareness. It was about 4 o'clock in the afternoon, sometime in May of 2002. I was observing very carefully the road and the surroundings, and was prepared to discover what I could see in the sky, in the trees, to what could appear just right in front of me. I was on Hacienda Road, going east, and turned left on Red-bud Rd. That was the road, in the car, hands on the wheel, I looked right in front of me, in the hills, and saw a huge dove etched onto the side of the hill, with unfolded wings and his head looking towards the East.

The last piece of the puzzle to reconstitute the inspired messages received from the Angels had been revealed! This dove was the missing link to guide me to relocate right here, in this city. Wow! I said. This is amazing as it gave me the validation of the inspired relocation. I looked at the dove and asked him what message he had for me. The feeling received was in relation to something in the further east, such as Las Vegas in Nevada, Phoenix or Tucson, in Arizona. When I spoke out loud each city to him, I received a feeling of a yes for Tucson, AZ. I thanked him with so much excitement and gratitude, and then I returned home. After parking my car in the back of my home, I looked towards the hills and realized that I could see the dove from there. What a thrill! I went to the front of my home and looked and saw an Angel on the San Jacinto Mountain. My body almost fainted from the overwhelming sensations. The Angel on the mountain is the same natural phenomenon as the dove, except it is even clearer, more precisely etched on the rock and it can be seen from miles away. I will tell you more about this angel in a chapter reserved for her.

The following Sunday, I went to church and asked if anyone knew of a dove and an angel in the direction of Tucson, Arizona. A charming lady by the name of Mary Frances looked at me and said "Well I got what you re looking for, I was born in Tucson. This is the White Dove. It's a church filled with wooden sculptured angels inside. I will bring you a book about it."

I was grateful for this validation in regards to the inspired messages I had received from the 'Dove'. I now knew that the next step was to go without procrastinating to the 'White Dove Church.'

CHAPTER TEN

THE MESSENGER

I have learned, through my own experiences, that when I receive a message from above, I have to act fast without postponing, otherwise it may be lost for a long time, or possibly forever. I would like to give you a few examples of this before I resume my story about my trip to The White Dove Church in Tucson, Arizona.

When I was a teenager, I often had visions and dreams. One of them occurred in the middle of the night around 4 o'clock in the morning. This is usually a favorite time for the Angels to send us inspired messages. A bright light came to my forehead and wrote a phone number that was from South of Paris with the first name, Vincent before leaving as fast as it came. The manner in which this bright light wrote those numbers reminded me of the beginning of the TV series 'The Mask of Zorro' when you see his sword writing Zorro. It was so shocking and real at the same time. I knew it was not a dream, but a message from above. A dream usually keeps going on once you start sleeping again, and can be confusing, with mixed things happening that don't often make sense. An angelic message comes as very distinct, shorter than a dream, and so much more precise. So precise, that I did not feel the need to get up in the middle of the night to write down those numbers, thinking I would of course remember them at dawn. It seemed that obvious. I remember telling myself that I would call these numbers in the morning and see if a Vincent lives there. I was so excited and could not wait for the morning to arise. When I woke up, I could not recall the last two numbers then the last four numbers the next day, etc. I regretted for a long time not to have gotten up to write them down. Who was that Vincent? Why was I given these numbers? I may never know.

Another time, when I was a child and still living with my family, I received in the middle of the night around the same time, an entire detailed description of a gentleman whom would be very important in the blooming of my career. I remember it very well. My heart was already in California at the time, but the state shown to me where this gentleman was living seemed to be somewhere close to the Canadian borders. I recall I was not happy about it, because it seemed that it was cold and rainy, like northern France where I was living, and I did not want to have to move to another cold region. Then from the state, the map zoomed in, to show me a city. I started to be intrigued and asked where in the city. Almost instantly, as if my thought triggered an instant response, it zoomed in again. I then asked if they could zoom in closer and I saw a village, then a house. From what I remember today, it felt like in the south west of that state. I could not see the gentleman but had a feeling of what his personality was. I was told that one day I will meet him and that he will be important in the start of my career. It could have been around Chicago, or Detroit, I am not sure. The thing is that at the time of its occurrence, it felt so explicit, and obvious that I would remember the entire message in the morning, as the details were so well–defined, but the truth is that I did not. For the second time, I had not written down the details and I missed the meaning of the message.

A third time, when I was a teenager, and living in Paris, I received the message that I had to go to Sevilla, in Southern Spain. There were not many details in this message except that it was clear that it was about meeting someone there. I never went to Sevilla, even though the message repeated itself several times in the middle of the nights. The pressure on my shoulder was persistent and I knew it would not quit until I had done it. However I did not. One day, it stopped so I knew that connection was gone. I had missed my chance to know why the Angels had insistently invited me to go. This is the reason why I also take the time and have the courage to share my personal stories with you, of how I could have done things differently or I could have listened more effectively and, most importantly, to teach you through my experiences to trust your inner voice, your intuitions and the message sent to you from the Divine. It is essential to blindly trust and do them, even when it makes no sense to you. You will know why you had to do it, after you have committed to do it first, with a blind faith. Now you understand more clearly why I went without any hesitation to Tehachapi and Caliente, California when I received the message of my relocation and why I could not defer that appointment with Spirit. I knew I had to go to Tucson, Arizona, after the message from the 'Dove' in the hills and the lady at my church who validated it. When you receive such a message, that you know comes from the Divine, it is a waste to either postpone or deny it. Furthermore, when I receive a mission to accomplish, the Angels usually keeps repeating it over and over, or it feels like they are after me all the time, behind my back, weighing on my shoulder, anything they can find to kick you to honor the mission until it is done.

I was on my way to Tucson a couple of days later and it took me almost 7 hours to get to this Franciscan Mission, south of Tucson, AZ. When I arrived, I went to the Priest's office where a secretary was working. I told her that I drove all the way from Palm Springs to talk to the Priest. She asked me what it was regarding. I just could not tell her. She seemed like a very rigid and firm person. I insisted, letting her know that I was here only for the next two days. She asked me to come back later as the Priest was out of his office right now. So I went to visit the 'White Dove of the Desert' as this place is also called. It is a small Catholic church founded in 1692 by a Jesuit Priest. This place is just amazing and overwhelming of artwork, such as wooden sculptured angels, paintings from different influences and of various religious figures. I sat on one of the church benches, and I prayed for the Angels to help me with my mission here, for everything to be fine. After the visit, I went back to the office and as the Priest was back, the secretary called him in. I told him that I had had a vision and I drove all the way to Palm Springs to talk to him, even though I did not know the reason why I had to do all this, and that all I was asking from him, was to be open and not judgmental about the whole thing, that I was not a crazy man. He responded calmly "Come to the mass tomorrow morning at 8:30 am, and after the mass you can talk to me before my next service." His response made me very pleased, as he was open to our encounter.

After mass the next day, like promised, he received me in his office. I told him once again that I had no idea why I was there and why I had to do all this, but I really felt God and the Angels put me on a mission, and that's why I ended up there in his office. I told him my story, the Near Death Experience at age 12, my move to America, and then about Palm Springs, the dove, and the angel which lead me to Tucson. He was listening to me very calmly, which was quite surprised. He was genuinely intrigued and interested in the stories and experiences that I was sharing with him. As I came to the end, his eyes released a few tears as he could relate to my story in its entirety, which led him to who he is today. A full circle had been completed by expressing my personal experiences as they helped him to release his own emotions for him heal and reconcile his past. He thanked me for telling him my story as it comforted him, knowing that he was not alone. When I left his office, the weight on my shoulder had vanished. This was the signal from the Angels that this mission was accomplished. It was then that I realized that the purpose of my trip to The 'White Dove' was for him.

This teaches us something very important about the messages from the Angels and the missions you may be presented with. Sometimes you may be called to do something that makes no sense to you, but when you listen and put the judgments aside, and do it with a total blind Faith, meaning that you may not know of the signification or the reason of the message until you actually honor it by completing the task. You do not bargain with God. You do not say "OK. I trust you, but first, give me this then I will do what you ask of me." You do it first with a blind trust in your Faith, and then after, you will receive your reward by knowing why you were called to do it, whatever it may be. This episode of blind Faith reminded me of a period of my life in my 20s when I realized that my presence sometimes was shaking things up. I remember several similar events when I was invited to visit some friends, which was a surprise by itself, to realize that a few weeks later the couple whom had invited me over, were breaking up. This happened so many times that I started to feel guilty, thinking I was causing this to occur and I could not understand why. Now, I understand that when living in the center of your heart, you radiate the truth that friends may feel the unconscious need to have you over so that it clarifies any secrets, darkness area in their relationship. I am happy to see that I am used this way, and it served the purpose for this trip to Tucson clarifying the Priest's life purpose.

CHAPTER ELEVEN

THE MIRACLES

When I arrived to Palm Springs in early 2002, the Angels put me on another mission. They told me that all I had to do was to find a place to give meditations, and that I would see.

First, I had to find a church. I remember a year earlier when I was still in Los Angeles I had a strong desire to play my music right after September 11, 2001 and asked different churches if they would like me to come play for them. The only one to welcome me to play was the 'Hollywood Church for Today' on Sunset Blvd in Hollywood, founded by Dr. Domenic A. Polifrone. He was such a great man and it was an honor to play in his Church. Thanks to him, I was able to participate in providing some comfort through the improvised music that I was letting my heart guide my hands to play, which I did throughout the day for anyone who wanted to pray and feel comforted by the soothing music. People were moved, just as I was, although it was sad to realize that it was only because of this tragedy that we were brought to feel as ONE.

I dream of a day when people start feeling responsible so we can feel and act connected as ONE without the need such tragedies to prompt it.

I was now new to Palm Springs and did not yet know anyone. Furthermore, I had never given any meditations in my entire life. I called several Christian churches, sincerely explaining who I was, with no success. Every time I wanted to perform in a Christian church, I was confronted with a series of questions as if I was at the Police Station being interrogated for being a suspect. It was frustrating. I thought "Why are these people so easy to judge me when they are supposed to preach the unconditional loving word of God?"

I remembered that the only church that had welcomed me in Hollywood, California was a Church of Religious Science which gave me the idea to contact one of the same in the Palm Springs area. One day, I knocked at the door of the Palm Springs Church of Religious Science without calling first. A charming lady, Dr. Reverend Florence Phillips, opened the door, as graciously as an angel would do. She said very nicely "Good morning Sir. What can we do for you?" I told her that I was a pianist and music composer and that the Angels told me to look for a place that would welcome me to give 'Healing Meditations with the Angels' and to try at your door. She suddenly shouted while singing to her husband, Dr. Reverend Ernest Phillips, who was in the church office "He is here, he is here. The one we were waiting for is here. The Angels have blessed us." This kind of shocked me at first as I did not know I was being waited for. She asked me to come in, closed the door and invited me over to their office. She acknowledged that they were currently looking for someone that would play music for their church services, and they were actually in the midst of writing a newspaper ad to look for a musician when I appeared knocking at their door. Perfect Divine synchronicity! This is the true Spirit orchestrating people and organizing with Spirit manner at Spirit speed. I love it. They welcomed me gracefully to do all that the Angels asked me to do. They also shared that they believed in the Power of God and the Angels and that their door was always open for me and my work. I was in awe in front of such an example of Grace. I had found people whom are genuinely preaching the word of God.

Back at home, I had to have a talk with the Angels. It is common for me to talk to them as if a human being was in the room. It's the same thing actually except that you cannot see them with your eyes. I told them "How am I going to do this? I have never given any meditations before. You are asking me to gather people in a Church while I have no idea what I am going to do." They responded with a smile "Yes, indeed. But you have nothing to worry about or to do except to bring your equipment and yourself. We will take care of the rest."

I was new in this area, and the idea of potentially making a fool of myself, was quite stressful. Was I forgetting that I needed to blindly trust and have Faith? Maybe my ego was afraid to see history repeating itself, by being humiliated or laughed at. At least, I was aware of the tricks of my ego, which is a good thing as it helps to release its seriousness and to laugh about it out loud.

I also asked the Angels "May I ask you something? May I ask you to rehearse just one time? I will visualize the audience and you work through me. Just to make sure we can do this together". They responded positively to this request and with a teasing smile, probably wondered "When is this guy going to relax?" I sat at my keyboard with headphones on to be in complete silence and with no distraction. I visualized the audience in front of me and I started to place my hands on the keyboard. My eyes closed, my voice started to speak to the virtual audience. It was a healing meditation to teach the audience how to feel worthy to surrender in order to receive any type of healing. It lasted about 40 minutes. I could not believe it. I had tears running down my cheeks as I was in total awe of what had just happened. I thanked them with the most grateful vibes from my heart and soul.

Then my ego took over again asking "What if it does not happen again the day of the meditation? How can I be sure?" The Angels had a hard time with me (smile). But I have integrity, and I am honest with myself and with you. That's why I am so open with you, and have the courage to narrate my personal stories; it is to tell you that it is okay to be doubtful or confused sometimes, as long as you are aware of the many tricks of the ego. The ego is not you. It wants to be you but it is not you. So each time the ego tries to take over to confuse you, please smile about it and do not take your ego so seriously. We will go into greater detail about the ego in another chapter. Also the reason why it is important for me to share all of these personal stories is that most of us get very impressed and may feel inferior in front of spiritual gurus, teachers, preachers, authors, etc thinking that they are superior, that they already know everything. This is not true. The spiritual teacher usually teaches what he needs to remind himself of doing. It serves you but it serves him at the same time. I am not any different. I am humble and honest enough to admit it. That is the difference. Someone who would make you feel inferior would only be coming from an egoistic place and that's not the kind of teacher you want to follow for your highest interest.

The day of the meditation had come. Fifty five people had come to see someone they had never heard before. I explained to them that I would surrender my ego in order to let Spirit come in to benefit all who were present, whatever that would be. I asked everyone to be as open as they could and not to judge any words that could be spoken during the meditation. I asked if anyone wanted to come up on stage. I had chairs behind my keyboard for anyone who wished to be in the energy of healing creation with the Angels. Four people came. I stood next to each of them, placed my right hand on their shoulder and the left hand directed towards the ceiling of the room, symbolizing the energy of the Angels, to receive specific messages for the person. Most of the time, the message was for the person to hold a thought or to focus at something during the entire meditation, a thought which usually would make no sense.

The Angels always say that if they were asking you to focus on something that you can understand, that makes sense, your brain would be in motion, and therefore the chance of you surrendering would be unlikely. By asking you to hold a thought that makes no sense to you, you do it emotionless since you cannot understand it, and therefore you are able to surrender with more ease, which enables the Angels to reach out to you with the needed Blessings. After repeating the same process with the three other people, I sat at my keyboard, put on my headphones and was able to proceed with the meditation.

From what I can remember, as each meditation is totally unique, it was done in 3 parts. I started to play the keyboard. I closed my eyes, and a few seconds later, the Angels started to speak through me. The first part was about acknowledging the elements of nature with pure love, the second, how to feel worthy to surrender and remembering what a beautiful soul we are, and the third was about all types of healing, and daring to give whatever was causing an imbalance to the Angels in order for the Angels to bless them. The meditation lasted an hour and a half.

My ego felt terrible and almost ashamed from not being able to recall whether it was good, effective or not. Typical of the ego to wonder this type of question! People seemed to have liked it and said that they felt very relaxed and some of them even said that they had never heard a meditation of this kind before. For the one channeling it, there is no immediate reward except for knowing that you allowed the Divine process to work through you to benefit others. I had no remembrance of anything that had been said, or of the music played, etc. Everybody said good-bye and left the church.

The Reverends that everyone referred to as "The Docs" were very pleased with the performance and they were always the sweetest with me. Dr. Florence, a lighthearted angel, was whistling and singing while putting the chairs back into place ready for the following Sunday service. I said good-bye and left.

I had not heard from them since the meditation. I finally decided to go to the Sunday service two weeks later. Mary Frances, who was the usher that day, shouted "Here is the miracle man, here is the miracle man!" "What miracle," I asked. "Well, you don't know, nobody told you?" she replied. Then I learned that 4 people on stage that evening two weeks ago had received Blessings. I have included a few testimonials from those who were touched by the Grace of God that night. Most importantly they had succeeded to surrender so the Blessings of Healing could reach them. The Angels always say that it takes only one second of surrender to be able to bring forth the miracle in you. Imagine, one second when your ego is out, you let go and surrender totally, in total bliss and blind Faith with God and the Angels to be blessed.

🕊 🕊 🕊 🕊 🕊 🕊 🕊

One lady's testimonial:

Dear Frederic, I want you to know how the healing has helped me. Over a year ago, I fell in a store, hurt my left shoulder. I had pain everyday. I have taken 3 or 4 aspirin at a time and a patch at night so I could sleep. Since the meditation, I am PAIN FREE and feel wonderful. Thanks again to you, God and your angels.

🕊 🕊 🕊 🕊 🕊 🕊 🕊

Second lady's testimonial:

Dear Frederic,
I was desperate for some peace and relaxation. I had had some severe back problems; in fact I had to close my catering business because of back pain due to misalignment and disc damage. At first I got into a very deep relaxed state. Then my body started to shudder and within a few seconds, my spine and all my joints felt completely aligned. According to my chiropractor, my back is in perfect condition and shows no signs of damage. Most important to me, I have been pain free since then. Thanks for your help, guidance and loving kindness.
May you have many, many, blessings.

🕊 🕊 🕊 🕊 🕊 🕊 🕊

Third testimonial from a gentleman who received the blessing of creation:

Frederic,
The last healing meditation I attended had some rather surprising re-
sults for me. I became so relaxed, and my head filled with such joy. I
slept 11 hours that night and the next morning I could play things on
the guitar I could not play before. Had attempted, but couldn't do but
now I can. So thanks to you for being the guide/channel/whatever
made that happen. All the best to you!

Fourth testimonial from a Reverend:

I recently attended Frederic Delarue's healing musical meditation. For
a period of several years, I have experienced a nagging pain in my lower
back that would at times be almost debilitating. Upon leaving the
church that evening I realized there was no longer any discomfort in
my back. Now I am still free of pain. I feel richly blessed by the healing
energy coming through Frederic to alleviate my pain. Rev. A.G.

Fifth testimonial from a friend:

One of the most wonderful events happened in this church.
I was always thinking of my grandma in Peru who passed away more
than a year ago. At that time, I could not leave the US to be close to her
for legal status. It hurt and I always felt guilty about it. During the
meditation I was having a lot of tears thinking of her. Then an amazing

revelation happened. My grandma came to a woman in the audience and asked her to deliver me the following message: 'I am happy and I am always with you.'

It was astonishing to hear that. It made me feel very happy and gave a huge relief from the guiltiness I was having.

Thanks to Frederic Delarue's musical healing meditation, my soul is healed.

As these testimonials illustrate, anything can happen. From a gift of creation, to a pain that is gone, to a damaged dorsal disk that is now normal, there is no limit to the Grace of God except for the ones that your mind may impose upon you. With God and the Angels, anything is possible!

After that day, we offered meditations frequently until the Docs graciously retired. I left the church with them, as the new board members at the time had no plans of continuing the meditations.

With God and the Angels, anything is possible for YOU too!

CHAPTER TWELVE

JESUS & HIS HEALING TEACHING

I was exhibiting, performing, and had been available as an Angel reader in some Body Mind Spirit Expos throughout Southern California during this period of time.

It was on this day, October 19, 2003, at the last Expo where I had participated located in the Scottish Rite Center in San Diego, California. On my way back to Palm Springs, I took State Route 79 Southbound instead of going North in the direction of home. I was so used to taking this route that I still don't understand why or how I took the route going the complete opposite direction. Again I surrender that everything happens for a reason. Prior to realizing that I was heading in the opposite direction, my first clue was that I noticed my car running out of gasoline. Surprised, I parked the car on the side of the road and turned it off, took a deep breath, and wondered what was happening. I immediately felt I had only two choices: continue forward which would make me take a huge detour through the Salton Sea before driving up to Palm Springs or turn around and try to reach the I-15. In either case, I felt I did not have enough gasoline. I took some time as I needed time to recompose myself. I prayed very strongly to God and the Angels and told them of the situation I had gotten into. The only reasonable choice was to go back towards the I-15 and I asked them to help me with the gasoline dilemma. I turned around and drove slowly. I prayed all the way, and by a miracle, made it to the next gas station close to the I-15. I had lost almost two hours and had almost two additional hours to get home. My car was loaded with my stuff for the Body Mind Spirit Expos, CDs, etc, as well as a small Angel statue that I had bought in a store in Palm Springs a few months earlier. I remember that day, when this Angel begged me to buy her. There were many angels displayed on a table. As soon as I had picked up the one that looked to be the most perfectly made, another angel caught my attention by popping up in my mind. I looked at her and noticed that she had many manufacturing flaws. She asked me to choose her with a very soft voice. I hesitated for some time before listening to the voice and taking her home with me. On my way back to Palm Springs, from San Diego, she was, of course in the car with me as I brought her with me to every Expo.

It was 11:53 pm and I was getting ready to take the very last exit from the freeway before reaching home, when something very strange happened. I passed a truck, and then I cannot remember anything after that except for the huge impact. I had lost consciousness and felt the sensation of a roller coaster. The shock was so brutal that I literally let go, thinking that was it for me, and I immediately surrendered entirely, as being ready to reach the Light for good this time.

The man in the truck later said that he saw my car hit the bridge railing near the wash on my right which propelled the car across 4 lanes of the freeway to the left, crossing them again to the right, and then finally rolling the vehicle over about 7 times before abruptly landing upright on its wheels. There was nobody on the freeway except for me and the truck I had just passed. He stopped and came to ask if I was okay and if there was anyone with me in the car. From the brutal shock, he thought the car might explode so he did not dare to come too close. He was shouting at me, to keep me awake. During this time I realized that I could not move. My hands were covered in blood and I said to myself "What did you just do?" I saw my cell phone on the floor that I tried to reach, in vain. The man from the truck, whom saved my life, called 911 and the ambulance quickly arrived. The paramedics talked to me to make sure I was responding and then asked me if I had a close friend to call. I gave them the phone number of Juan-Carlos, whom at the time, was living two hours away. They asked me things like: what is your name and who was the President of the United States, etc. to keep my mind busy and avoid a loss of consciousness. They carefully put on a neck collar, and placed me onto a board before sliding me into the ambulance. They transported me to the Desert Regional Center Medical Center in Palm Springs. Inside the emergency room, they were talking, laughing, and joking. I understood that seeing the most horrible bloody scenes arriving in the ER all the time, their job is not an easy one and they used jokes and laughter in order to relax and remain sane.

A male nurse started to wash my hands while talking and joking with his colleagues and it hurt like hell as he was washing off the blood, sand, dust, and pieces of glass that were inside of my wounded hands. I could not move my neck and could barely speak. A lady approached me on my left and asked me if

I had insurance, if I believed in God, and which church I belonged to. I thought, what a cool time to ask me so many questions. Regarding my answer to which church I belonged to, I said the church of religious science, which was the only church that welcomed me to play my music without any conditions. When she asked me my religion I simply answered "Spiritual". She asked me again, and I repeated "Spiritual". She asked me again by mentioning all of the denominations of religion such as Christian, Protestant, Presbyterian, Unitarian and so forth but Spiritual was not on her list, so she wrote 'other'. Since Spiritual may mean all religions together for unlimited love, there could not have been a box for it, as a box is by itself a limitation of thought. This ultimately made me smile internally.

Juan-Carlos arrived just a few hours after receiving the phone call, and I was nicely surprised to see him arrive so soon. It felt so nice to have his friendly presence at that moment. I asked him if he could go check my totaled car for any personal objects. He called the church for help and a few members kindly took their time to go to the scene and gather all the objects spread out at the site of the accident. They found absolutely everything that was in the car, from pens, money, CDs, business cards, brochures, boom box, etc., except for one thing. The Angel! I figured the Angel had sacrificed herself for me. Most amazingly, the accident happened on vacant land from where you can see 'the Angel on the mountain', in Palm Springs. I leave you with your thoughts on that.

Both of my hands, face and hair were badly ravaged by a multitude of pieces of glass, sand dirt and blood. I could not move my hands anymore which felt heartbreaking for a pianist. However the doctors were more concerned about my lungs which were both punctured, and they were getting ready to take further action in case my condition got any worse.

I would like to take a moment now to explain that two days prior to this accident, my nephew, Charles, who was 10 at the time, had received visions about a man, whose head he could not see, lying in a emergency room with doctors on one plane of the room and two enormous Angels with golden wings with diamonds on both side of this man. These Angels were actively working to heal him. My nephew told his mom, who is also my sister, about this, as he could not understand the vision. This vision repeated a couple of times. When they learned about my accident a few days later, my nephew understood that the Angels he had seen before the accident physically happened were for his Uncle Frederic and saw that this man, who he now knew was me, would be saved by these magnificent Angels.

The doctors came back to my room after several X-Rays and said it was a miracle because my punctured lungs amazingly started to heal, which was rare. I gave thanks to the Angels. My nephew shared with me later on, that he had never seen such beautiful Angels in his entire childhood. They were so tall, beautiful and had huge golden wings covered with many diamonds.

The next day after the accident, from my hospital bed, I asked God and the Angels what happened, and something odd started to occur. Jesus suddenly appeared in my room, like the special effects in the movie Star Wars, and said to me "Hold my hand, and come with me. I want to show you something." One second after, we were at some place in the desert and he said "Walk up that hill on your left and watch, enjoy and learn." There were other people on that hill to the left also waiting. Jesus went towards the right to His place of healing where a huge crowd of thousands of suffering people had gathered down below. Jesus took His place, beautiful and radiant as always. His aura was so brilliant, like rays of sunlight reaching out from behind cotton clouds or like rays from Heaven. His extra luminous aura radiated about 40 feet in diameter. It was impressive to witness.

Those who were ill, waiting in line to receive the promised healing from Jesus, looked in much pain, some were crying, screaming and suffering, while others were lamenting of deep sorrow and despair. As soon as they entered into the healing aura of Jesus, their bodies would shake and tremble as they instantly weakened, some fell to their knees, as if by magic, and in this moment of surrender, they were already giving their power and pain away to God while in His incredible presence of Loving Light. The other people on the hill who had been watching the healing scene with me, started to take their place in line. I followed them and my turn soon came. I knelt down from the Power of His brilliant aura that instantly weakened my body. I was letting go and surrendering without knowing it. My head bowed facing the soil. He reached for my face with His hands so I could look at Him, touched my forehead, and then with my cheeks in His hands, He said to me "Now you know, my friend, how Miracles occur with your music. Be at peace with it. Accept it fully and know that I am with you. Go with no fears of what you do." He then released His hands from my cheeks and allowed me to go.

This scene of Jesus healing people will remain with me forever. When He first came into my room and asked me to follow Him, He was already so beautiful. But while He was at work, He immediately developed that immense Light, like He was the sun and rays of light were emanating, radiating from Him. His words of wisdom were incredible to me, as I had always wondered how healing could take place while I was giving the Musical Meditations in the Church in Palm Springs. His aura, so intense and powerful created a sacred space of loving Light where people had no other option than to surrender and kneel before Him, in order to be blessed. This is how the luminous presence of His aura prepared them for their healing, and then He finished the process by placing His healing hands on them. The same thing happens with the music that Spirit flows through my hands, a sacred space is created where the listener can surrender to the power of soothing music to fully receive their blessings.

When I was a child, raised as a Catholic, there came the time to do my communion. I never really understood why there were so many rules and rigidity attached to the church. We were required to spend an hour a day with the priest for several months. Also, having to kneel to the Virgin Mary did not make sense to me. In my innocence, I asked the Priest, and let's just say the question was not well received. I remembered all the wonderful moments that I spent with God when I was walking in nature alone or with my dog. I could be humble and respectful without being imposed to kneel. So little by little, all these unnecessary rules and austerity pushed me away from Religion, as it did not resonate with my heart. However, after that very special night when Jesus came to me, took my hand, and invited me to watch Him, the one I had always imagined in my mind and felt in my soul, the one that unconditionally loves everyone without any judgment helped me to reconcile with Him.

If this was the only reason for having had this accident, the blessings that I received that night were well worth it and I am eternally grateful to Him for that.

A friend came to pick me up at the hospital when I was released four days after the accident. It was a strange feeling as I was re-discovering people, walking, running, the homes, the cars, everything. I was not happy to be back. I thought it was odd the way we all have our little cars to move from one place to another. It felt so outdated. I was wondering why we were not moving with other ways of transportation, such as teleportation, etc. It felt like we were using so much energy for very inefficient ways to transport ourselves or do anything. This feeling lasted for at least a couple of weeks. Every morning I would look at the beautiful view of my place, and I was not happy to be back. I was questioning "Why am I back? What kind of world is this? I don't like it. I want to go home." When I tell this part of the story during conferences and concerts, many come to me and ask "You say you did not want to be back. Didn't you feel sorry to die and leave your parents? Didn't you miss them? Didn't you care for them?" Of course, I cared for my family. This is, of course, a controversial issue for most of us, whom have learned to live through the control of attachments. Our Society taught us from early age, that this is be 'my' toy, 'my' food, 'my' plate, 'my' job, 'my' car, 'my' house, 'my' wife, 'my' children, and these attachments becomes therefore 'my' hell! Anybody who is afraid of death, and thinks that death is the end, would ulti- mately experience these emotions of attachment, based on the fear of losing life and the refusal that we are not a soul in the first place. Life cannot end. Life just is! It is only experienced on dif- ferent levels.

The doctors had released me from the hospital. However, my hands were still badly injured. Pieces of glass were still under the skin on the top of my hands, near the tendons of my fingers. Concerned that the pieces of glass may do more damage to my fingers, I asked the doctors to remove them. They refused think- ing that I was making a big drama out of nothing. Meanwhile, my left hand was healing very well and so fast that you could barely see where the injuries were. My right hand was strug- gling and refusing to heal because of the significant pieces of glass that were still sitting right next to the tendons of my mid- dle finger. Concerned that I may never be able to play the piano again, and because of their refusal to take care of me, I was trying to find a way to request all the medical files from the accident. That is procedure normally used when you want to file a lawsuit against a hospital. However, my goal was not to sue them but to put pressure on them to get them to do something. The rehabilitation doctors were actually forcing me to move my fingers and tried to convince me that the pieces of glass would eventually end up coming to the surface of the hand before leaving the body.

It went on like this for many weeks and I knew it was not right. Out of despair, I called a producer I knew and told him the story. He immediately wrote a letter to the hospital and a few days later, I received a call saying that they were sending me to a hospital in Fontana in San Bernardino County, for further evaluation. When I arrived to the Hand Specialist, he was shocked to see that a big chunk of glass was sitting on top of my tendons. He actually could not believe the Hand Specialist in Palm Springs had refused to remove them and even worse, forced me to practice moving my hands, which could have ultimately caused the tendons to be cut. A few days later, the Hand Specialist from the Fontana Hospital performed surgery on my right hand, removed all the pieces of glass and gave them to me as a souvenir.

My hands healed well and after some tough rehabilitation I was able to play again, and more beautifully than ever, as my hands now have the Light of Jesus in them.

CHAPTER THIRTEEN

RELIGION PARADOXES

Even though this chapter may be controversial for some of you, I find it essential to share the facts from my personal experiences with Religion. Their impact on me and the acknowledgment of my higher purpose for being, in the course of my life, from a child to my adult life, and who I am today, is indisputable.

As a child, I continually heard the Priest giving orders to kneel to the statues representing the Virgin Mary or to Jesus without giving any explanation other than I had to out of respect. We were not allowed to talk in the church, or to feel happy and had to pretend to be in this continuous state of seriousness, probably to show respect as well. In a child's heart, it was difficult to understand why God, Jesus or even Virgin Mary would want the ambiance to be so somber. I could not comprehend why we could not rejoice and celebrate what was in our hearts as children.

It felt a disconnection between life and the church. On one side there is life with the birds, the blue sky, the clouds, the wind, the rain, the sunshine, the laughter, and the joy within. On the other, there was the church where everybody put on a sad face, as if we were living an endless funeral. The submissive side of it was not resonating with any of the children around me and the result would be totally opposite of what the Priest expected from us. Instead of understanding, obeying and being part of it, we were laughing and making jokes about it as his request and behavior seemed so absurd. As children we were still living in our hearts and expressing the joys of life.

Throughout my years as a teenager, I was the only pianist in town. I was hired by the Priest to play the organ at all the churches in the many villages near my home, for Sunday services and also for special occasions, such as weddings, funerals, and baptisms. During this time, I witnessed and heard a lot of negative comments from the Priest whom was in charge of the village and other churches in the surrounding areas however, I chose to hush up. He seemed like an angry, musty man and his congregation, which would only come for special occasions, such as weddings and funerals, were not being duped. From witnessing unethical practices such as the gold disappearing from the church, which was sold to antique stores in the area by the Priest himself, to emotionless readings of the Bible, and other inappropriate and judgmental gossips, I was not too impressed. It felt like a disconnection somewhere between the teaching and the heart.

Other experiences, such as in Medjugorje, Bosnia-Herzegovina, reflected the echoes of discontinuity between the original purpose and reality. The Church, without mentioning a recipient, publishes the Virgin Mary's message that is often about inviting us to pray for peace. Paradoxically to that, you may often hear unloving and violent words of hatred. I recall one afternoon when I heard straight from a Sister's mouth, that all gays, lesbians, thieves, gangs, drug addicts, prostitutes, psychics, healers, mediums, and so forth, were people of Satan and that if we knew any of them, first we had to cut off all links with them and secondly, to report them with names and addresses to the many Priests lined up in the booths. I also wondered why this Sister, who had taken a name similar to Mother Theresa, had chosen to speak her version of the 'Word of God!?' I ask you the reader: How could her request have come from All Mighty God?

On one hand, you come to Medjugorje for peace, healing, and the Virgin Mary, and you leave with the word of Satan expressed hundreds of times. Again understand this is not a judgment, but an unfortunate real experience that I have witnessed. I intentionally have refrained from interjecting further details and just keep to the facts.

Most recently, a French Priest from a famous pilgrimage town in the South of France chose to judge me on many levels without ever meeting me in person. He used words such as 'pure wind', 'falsely angelic being', 'abusing people', 'void music', 'dangerous mystic figure', etc. I wonder from what he based his conclusion...

These facts that speak for themselves have contributed to turning me away from organized Religion, but not from my beliefs in God, in Jesus or in Mary, not from my Great Faith, not my discernment from within, or my own Truth. I am, however, saddened by the fact that some Preachers and Sisters speak words of hatred and lower themselves to profanity through their unjustified judgments in the name of Jesus.

I have always believed that there is a good in each and every one of us and that we all wish to be loved for who we are, and who we are resides in the depth and warmth of our loving hearts. Anytime our heart has been betrayed and/or hurt, we have the choice once again to decide what to do. We can take revenge and perpetuate this hurt to others, which is the most common, or take responsibility by recognizing our connection with God, Jesus, and forgive unconditionally. I see that many times during private sessions with families that have struggled with abusive behaviors for decades or even centuries is continuing because they do not know any better than to repeat the same vengeances, the same wars, the same patterns, as this is all they have known. It is not until one member of this family wakes up and takes responsibility to cut these ties from this cycle of abuse once and for all, that they will finally be free. When someone succeeds to do this, I know they have God, Jesus within.

As I mentioned previously, the day after the 9/11 tragedy, I felt deeply moved to play my music for people, and offered to perform at many Christian and Spiritual Churches in the Hollywood area. The only one that responded with a positive attitude and without conditions was the Hollywood Church of today founded by Dr. Domenic A Polifrone. In general, it feels odd, to say the least, that some Churches seemed more pre-occupied to judge whether I was a good Christian than to allow me to perform with a loving heart. I guess everyone has their own priorities and mine are to speak from my heart and this is exactly what happened on that night after my car accident on October 20, 2003 when I had reconciled with Jesus, and felt the overwhelming peace of a loving parent.

I long for a world where we all respect each other's breath of life, a world where Peace reigns, of a Religion that links, unites and embraces all people, our many differences, and our hearts and souls.

I have a complete blind faith in God, and total trust in the guidance I have received from the Angels. It took me clarity and discernment to stay grounded to become who I am today. I wish everyone could have the opportunity to see through the clarity of their own hearts.

I invite you to do a few simple exercises that may help you to develop clarity within, intuition, and inner voice. Learn to listen to your body as it helps you to discern between what's real and false. We usually sense very well between the truth and a lie when we listen to the muscles of our stomach, when it suddenly finds itself blocked or when it feels at peace, which we interpret as right. But do we trust our feelings? Or do we prefer to live by and trust what others have told us to believe? Do we wish to feel our own truth or to feel what others convince us to feel as our truth? In other words, do you choose to live your own life or the life of someone else? The Society we live in likes to decide pretty much everything for us.

For you to be successful at this exercise I invite you to be open and play as fair as you can in this spirited game of imagination and visualization.

Here is an example: We as a Western cultured Society often impose upon other civilizations, our cultures with its rules and laws as if we were already living in a dictatorial One World Order. What if the indigenous Etoro tribe from Papua New Guinea or China had power over the Earth, and therefore would impose their cultures, their rules and laws to all of us in the Western world. Would you like this to happen? Would you think it's fair? Why impose on others what we would not appreciate to have done to ourselves?

I thank you in advance for doing the following exercise with me as I acknowledge it takes a lot of courage to be open to see our anchored beliefs amid controversy.

Imagine, just for one moment that you are an Atheist, and I dare to tell you that God visited me last night and now I know that my calling is to go help people in Rwanda. How would you feel about what I just proposed? The probability is that you, as an Atheist, might think I am just a nutcase, or even worse, dangerous, just because you do not believe in God and that 'calling' refers to nothing within the parameters of your understanding. Why might you think that? Because it would potentially disturb your beliefs, the very foundation of what your life is based upon. You may find that what disturbs your strong beliefs may be judged as dangerous, as it is part of the 'unknown' world, for you.

This next exercise is even more controversial. The reason is to provoke you and invite you to debate a polemical and disputative subject to open it up for discussion, to expand your mind, and broaden your thoughts that you may rarely question. You may be living and thinking on auto pilot or have mistaken whatever has been imposed on you as your own truth. Have you not ever caught yourself doing something in a robotic manner? You just do things because that's all you know. You don't even question it. The same applies to other cultures that teach their youth to wear machine guns. They don't question it because it is all that they know. Other beliefs, regarding religion or not, may have also been taught to you as being the truth, which you don't question either because that's all you know. Think about that in your spare time. It's incredibly healing and expanding to allow yourself to see your life from different perspectives.

In our Western culture, we often hear people talk about God or the Christ as if they really know who they are. In reality you talk about God and Jesus with a blind Faith and trust that they exist. You do not have proof other than reading about them in the Bible, unless you have met with them, during a NDE, or a similar situation in a spiritual manner. Without being offensive, the Bible was written and re-written and translated, and re-translated, and re-adapted and re-adjusted and similarly, every human being has learned to adjust to what they understand, they know of, or they believe and consequently, want others to believe too. It all comes down to the perception we have from things or events, once more.

Let's do another exercise together. Imagine that I dictated on a digital recorder what is to be a book containing the new Bible, a book of prophecies for the next 900 years to come. Your task is to listen and write it down for the generations to come. In it are many sentences and topics that are in total opposition with your current beliefs. What would you do? Would you be honest enough to write it exactly the way I dictated it, or would you distort it just a little bit so it corresponds best to remain within the comfort zone of your beliefs?

I am only daring to push this example a step further to take you out of your comfort zone to expand your awareness of your most treasured beliefs for you to determine if they are truly your own beliefs or those of someone else.

Our thoughts become our beliefs and in turn create the reality of our life. If I had kept thinking that I would never be able to go to America, it would have created my beliefs, and therefore physically manifested my chosen reality to never being able to do it. However I chose to think that I would be going to America one day, which created these positive beliefs, and made it my current reality. It is as simple as that.

When you allow yourself to open up to this type of exercise without judgments or pre-conceived beliefs, you then develop your inner ability to have clarity on things, on events, on discernment, on who you truly are, and on the powerful and beautiful soul being that you are.

I took the chance to give you these exercises to help you to find clarity within yourself, reconnect with the true wonderful soul that you are, and to re-claim your powers back. Not that you do not have power now, but I am a believer that our mind can do so much more than what we have taught it to do. Our mind has infinite powers that have been programmed by society to not use or re-awaken; otherwise no one could have any control over us. This is just something else for you to think about.

When you succeed to accomplish this, you are empowered with such a greater force, strength, and faith, and nothing, nobody, no limitations or restrictions can prevent you from growing and glowing in your own Light.

CHAPTER FOURTEEN

LIFE PURPOSE

After encountering the Angels and acknowledging them in my presence during a NDE at the age of 12, I have continued to communicate with them throughout my life. Amazingly enough, they saved me two more times: once when I was paralyzed after a surgical mishap, and the other, during the last car accident when Jesus appeared to me.

At first glance, the NDE appeared to be a terrible accident however it was actually the most beautiful blessing in disguise I had ever received. Being paralyzed could have destroyed me mentally, yet it strengthened me because I saw in this incident the good message that God had sent me. I had been running away from my path, so I had to be stopped, and being paralyzed was one way to force me to regroup my true Self. Also totally accepting the fact that I may be paralyzed for life, and having no emotional attachment to it, may have contributed to my rapid and miraculous healing. The last accident could have been disastrous as well. Yet the Angels saved me and trusting the episode that followed the event with Jesus appearing to me were two blessings in one. This is the way I choose to see everything in life.

I am grateful for all of these events, and for choosing to accept with total faith the experiences brought to my awareness such as the Presence of the Angels, the Beings of Light, and Teachings of Healing with Jesus. I have allowed myself to see the bigger picture from a detached perspective, and seeing beyond the physical and emotional attachments and barriers. I was able to surrender, follow the guidance received, and have clarity and discernment through love, inner peace, gratitude and the acceptance of each moment. Acceptance is probably one of the most important things to honor; accepting everything that comes to your life knowing there is a greater reason for it. Again it always comes back to pure total and blind faith, regardless of the denomination of your religious or spiritual beliefs. Everyday of your life sees your faith tested. Do you believe and send Love to God when everything turns out the way you decided it should, and start blaming Him when things do not turn out the way you or your ego would have wanted? "How big is your faith?"

Appearance and superficiality... do you attest to these illusions? We are all aware of the oasis of water appearing off in the horizon on a hot summer day. Is it real, or just a mirage? Things aren't always as they appear. What may first seem as an unfortunate or negative event may turn out to be the greatest blessing that God has ever sent you! Be patient and let the blessing unfold. If you judge, blame and refuse to accept the lessons, experiences and events that God has mysteriously placed in the sequence of your life to serve your Highest Purpose; you will end up playing the victim with all the emotional consequences attached to it.

However if you choose to fully accept and embrace every lesson, experience and event, even if it is not pleasant or does not make sense at the time of its occurrence, and have total blind faith, you might end up seeing the Blessings out of the torment. Sometimes you may have to lose one thing to gain another.

Let's take several examples to demonstrate this. Imagine getting laid off from work. At first glance, this appears like a terrible thing, because of an immediate loss of money that will result from it, triggering panic and emotional stress. It may also be for the loss of something you were attached to and probably even worse, that you were identifying yourself with, 'your job'. Confusing who you are with the job that you were doing is a loss of your own identity. Depression may follow from this delusion and misperception of defining yourself as your job. In this case, referring to it as 'your' job as something that you possess or you own, is a misconception in itself. A job is only a trade, and the work consists of a physical or intellectual energy that you give in exchange for another type of energy, called money. You cannot be your job, nor your car or anything that you have the illusion to possess. The feeling of depression often comes from the emotion linked to an illusionary attachment.

What if God had a greater plan for you through the loss of this job? What if this lay off was in fact the greatest opportunity that the Universe had sent you to give you all the time needed to finally take care of yourself, and most importantly, to honor your natural gift(s). You may know, or not, of a natural talent that you have, whether it is writing, playing music, comedy, acting, painting, singing, dancing, sculpting, inventing, and so forth, yet because of the lack of time due to the job you were already doing, you were not able to either explore it or honor it. What if God had sent you this loss so you can gain a better job that best suits your life purpose, the one of your passion, the one of your heart?

Now you may say to yourself "OK but how will that bring me sufficient money to live or fulfill the needs of my family?" All of these answers reside in the depth of your heart and faith of your soul. If you honor the gift of God, (your God given talent), and do it with a pure heartfelt passion, it will come back to you in a beautiful and unexpected manner.

An example would be that God is talking to you and screaming "You are a great painter, try it. Do it. I love you. Trust yourself and just do it." However you do not hear His voice because you have been too busy in the midst of the stormy egoistic depression you are in, after losing a job.

Let me give you two different perspectives, one from a Christian point of view and the other is Spiritual. If you choose to listen to the voice of God, your intuitions, your inner voice or the Angels, either of the following will be your reward.
As a Christian believer, God will be so happy to see you honoring the gift He gave you that He will reward you with many blessings, including financial energy. As a Spiritual believer, by honoring your inner God given gift, the Universe will bring you more of what you had sent out. So in other words, if you trusted your gift and honored it, the Universe can only send you more of what you sent out, which is more work through trusting the process and honoring your God given gifts that will manifest in a return of financial energy as well. You see, in both scenarios, the result is essentially the same. The only difference is how you choose to perceive it.

Having an attachment to things blocks you from seeing with the eyes of your heart. Again, let me repeat that you are not to be attached to any thing. You are not your car, your job, your house etc. You are a beautiful soul that came on earth for a specific mission and you are being given tools, such as job, car, house, etc to bring it to completion with the most ease and happiness. Remember, you are a Spiritual Being living a human experience, and the connectivity you have with The Source, whatever that is in your understanding and level of awareness, is your connection to get you through this Life.

What follows is my understanding of the messages that I have received from the Angels, and is not an attempt to impose on you any other belief than your own. As a soul living a human experience, I apply what I have learned, with love, inner peace, acceptance, gratitude and surrender of our differences. I am inviting you to be open to what follows with a warm heart. What makes us evolve is the acceptance and gratitude of our differences, and to surrender, detached of your human limitations and beliefs and I thank you for that.

Angels have shared with me that our soul, which is what we are and will always be, accepts to come to earth with a purpose, an exploration, experience or experiment, depending on our chosen mission. We also decide when we wish to come back and choose the most appropriate family for the lesson to be learned. We live until our body dies, which then liberates the soul from our physical body. After this happens, we then have the opportunity to review every event and lesson we experienced in our life. By doing this we will be able to see the choices that were made in our highest interest and those that we could have done differently. This continues to unfold until the soul is purified of it all. Death is really just the beginning of another birth. Like a tree that dies so one of his seeds can be reborn and grow into another tree, which will also die so another seed can grow, and the cycle of life continues. Our soul can also choose to come back again for the next mission, by planting another seed, if it feels that additional learning on earth would be helpful. In each life we gather a piece of the larger puzzle, (the bigger picture) that may form a full circle one day, which is what we refer to as ascending. In this case, coming back may not be necessary.

Angels also say that sometimes some of them accept to see their high vibrations lowered to take a human appearance in order to bring forth help and clarity among others.

We are a soul above all else and live on earth as Spiritual Beings living a human experience, rather than a human being having a spiritual experience. When you really understand the difference, your life and the perception of your life may shift instantly.

In each lifetime lived, we are invited to explore, experience or experiment the lessons that are to be learned. The mission can be anything and all missions are important and are not to be judged as one being better than any other. Some may choose to raise a family, and the children who choose them as parents will bring forth their lessons to be learned in this lifetime. The children may end up being the teacher of their parents and vice versa as their lessons will happen simultaneously. Some may choose to open people's hearts through any type of artistic career, while others may be gifted for Justice, and they will wish to become a lawyer, or to help to heal their brothers and sisters by honoring a medical career, and so forth. We come here as equal and what our ego and mind makes of us is a different matter.

We, as a soul, also decide when we wish to come back on earth. Angels say that we chose what era we want to explore a situation. For example, if the mission to be explored and learned is to provide peace you may decide to come back at a time of war. If you choose to come back to learn from peace, you may choose to explore to be what we call on earth 'the bad guy' in order to learn how to receive peace, unconditionally.

We choose the most appropriate family for the lesson to be learned. This statement may stir up controversy for some of you who read this. During my childhood and adolescence, I used to hear people say that we choose our friends, not our family which could explain why most of us don't get along with our families. The ego in that case is happy as a King could be, as all the blame is directed towards the so-called un-chosen family. Are you playing the victim again, or do you believe God created you in His image? If He did, then accept all that is, including your family as being the best one to fulfill the lessons in your life to be experienced for your life's purpose and Divine plan.

It makes more sense that we pre-select our family since we will more likely learn from the various experiences we have with them. It might not be easy but that's what needs to be embraced with full acceptance, gratitude and surrender for the lessons to be learned. Changing your name for the reasons to dissociate yourself from family may take you away from you path and who you are, and refusing your family entirely may do the very same. However you may not always agree with every member of the family that you choose. Angels reassure you. Am I seeing a smile of relief in your face now? (Smile) As a soul, you can have a wide vision of anything anywhere, and therefore it is easy for a soul to pinpoint which person may assist them in their life's mission. Once found, we might come back to experience another lifetime just for that person to help them complete some unfinished lessons. They could be anyone in our circle, such as is a family member, so you could either come back just for the mother, the father, a niece, a sister, a brother, a nephew, and so on.

When my nephew was born in 1993, I was guided to write a long letter to my sister, his mom, to share with her the mission of his life and what he will be going through and what he needs to learn. It was flowing as easily as when the music flows through my hands. His first year was a delicate balance between life and death, and when he chose to stay, I knew that we would become closer after he turned 14. However the Angels prepared him sooner by sending him visions of them performing a healing on me during my last car accident when he was 10. He came to this life with some physical challenges that he needs to learn to accept, be grateful knowing there is a reason for them, and to surrender to the power of God, the Angels and himself in order to claim a potential miracle. Knowing fully that before he came into this life with the physical issues he would be facing on earth, he chose a family where one member could ease his task. This is where I come into the picture as I have already opened the path for him by doing the major work to live in the US. I know he might be called to follow the same path to help others through the difficulties of his childhood and adolescence.

The key for healing is the acceptance and the surrender of all the events we are going through, with gratitude. If it becomes a battle, like in every war, there are always losers in every camp. So this is not a path I like to choose.

We live our life until our body dies, which liberates the soul from our physical body. This refers back to the first Chapter where it is explained that during a Near Death Experience, the body may either die clinically or die totally, in case of real death. Understand, however, that death is only the beginning of another birth. During the NDE, my body died clinically which liberated my soul to fly anywhere at a fast pace and with much ease and happiness while having a global vision of everything. I found that the physical body often limits us from seeing beyond our physical eyes, the body limits us from flying, from having a different perspective, or angle about our life. For example, when you feel stressed out, you see the struggle that you are faced with, your little world, your selfish misery, as it seems you are the world of suffering, and nothing else matters. It can be a beautiful day outside, the birds may be singing, and God may be sending out many messages to you that you will automatically miss, just because you limited yourself to see and live in your own little world. Once your body dies, the soul is free to fly and have a wide vision of everything on the planet and beyond.

The key to being able to have the same clarity during your living existence is to succeed in detaching yourself from your physical limitations and using your mind to visualize the scene where you are from different angles of the room you are in. For example, imagine you are sitting in your bedroom feeling stressed. Visualize flying, as if your soul is free and is able to see your stressed body, the material, physical you, the color of your vibration expressing your current state of being, from every angle above the room. Watch and feel yourself without judging. Compare this to your neighbor's homes. Doing this exercise, you may even receive essential messages for your physical body. It takes practice to do this well, but it is totally possible. When I find myself stressed, and allow myself to watch my body from above, I usually find myself saying "What are you doing?" and I laugh out loud at the situation I dared to put myself into.

Again, it all comes down to: "Do you really believe in God? Do you really trust God?" If the answer is yes, then what are you worrying about? If God is perfect and you are created in

His image. He knows what He is doing, and the lessons to be learned. So you are taken care of.

What matters is not how many times you go to church but how many times you have a blind Faith in God even when the toughest situations occur. When you are in a difficult situation, you have the choice to accept it and embrace the lesson no matter how hard it may be to go through. You can choose to even be grateful of the situation, and surrender to the Ultimate Power of God. This will find you succeeding and healing.

My life Purpose was revealed at an early age when I started to learn piano. I was blessed through the NDE at the age of 12 by receiving the gift to help people feel better and reconnect with their true self through the power of soothing music flowing from my heart to my hands.

Again, I am reminded of Mr. Secondé who drew my Aura, showing my past lives as a healing masseur in Egypt and a devoted women musician in a Greek monastery playing spiritual music. They are now combined as my current Life Purpose; a spiritual composer who massages people's souls by reconnecting them, and most importantly, reconciling all the pieces of their true Self through the Power of Soothing Music.

CHAPTER FIFTEEN

THE POWER

OF

SOOTHING MUSIC

Music has always been a part of my life. This is the living vibration that keeps me alive. I feel whole when I play and create music or to be more exactly, when I let Spirit create the masterpieces through me, as a vessel. As a child and teenager, I considered that music was the center of my life. I even wrote one of my first songs at the age of 19 with the name: "Music is my life" with lyrics such as "I am married with my music."

Music is sound. Music is vibration. Music is energy. Music is Universal. I hear music everywhere, as everything is energy, and/or vibration. Everything vibrates in this universe, and vibrations create sounds, and sounds are music for the soul. For instance, the sounds of birds singing and conversing with each other may inspire. Have you ever heard the sounds in the vibration of colors, textures, scents, touch, love making, dance, and of course voice and music?

In a world like ours, when everything goes so fast, do you take the time to listen to the vibration of your body, the sounds within your body, and what these sounds may be telling you? Do you take the time to touch the body of a tree, listen to his vibrations, feel his music of the wind in his leaves, and of your hands conversing with his body? Do you take the time to caress a flower and feel its music, the music of its colors, its texture, and smell? Do you take the time to listen and to feel the power of Silence, its music, the density of its vibration? Do you take the time to caress your body, to feel the sound and the vibration when you touch your body when it is wet, and dry? Do you take the time to feel the music in the rain, in the wind, in the snow, in the sand, in the water, in the air? Do you take the time to look at a tree for a long time, converse with it as you would with a friend, and hear the vibration, the aura, the power, the music that radiates from this tree to you, and feel your power emanating love towards this tree? Do you take the time to feel the music of love, the music of forgiveness? Do you take the time to feel the power of soothing music, and breathe it in as a source of power to re-awaken all of the sleepy and/or unbalanced cells in your body? Do you take the time to listen to the vibration of the water you drink and the food you eat every day while traveling its course within your body? Do you take the time to listen to your body when you eat healthy food vs. junk food? Do you take the time to feel the vibration of your soul? Do you take the time to feel you? Do you take the time to honor you? Do you take the time to love you?

Do you take the time to listen to you?

When you allow yourself to be in complete silence and calmness, you will be amazed at all the sounds of music that you will hear. The messages that you will be receiving is the key. Will you trust them or judge them?

Let me retrospect a little what has already been said in a previous chapter. As a young child, I learned that music could heal my sadness in just in a few minutes by playing whatever was flowing through my hands. I was releasing any negative tensions, just like that, through the power of soothing music. When I had the privilege to play the Great Organs of Chartres and Lisieux, and at the Gallardon Church in France as a teenager, it was an exquisite sensation to feel the power of the sounds vibrating in the Cathedral throughout my entire body! Without forgetting the feeling while taking the old steps to the Great Organ such as the smell of humidity in the old wood, from the vibrations, the energy of that place, and the sounds of wood cracking under my feet.

From the age of 5 thru 15, my piano teacher, Miss Couturier, introduced me to the soft emotions of Claude Debussy. I found his music very different from any other Classical Composer. Among my favorites are Claude Debussy, Gabriel Fauré, Maurice Ravel, Sergei Rachmaninov, and Erik Satie. What I loved most about Debussy's compositions is that each note of his many masterpieces, are played with emotion, intention, and with subtlety in the intensity of each gentle sound. What intrigued me was how a single note could sound so differently, depending on the intention you were sending out from your heart, to your fingers, which would consequently and immediately fulfill the listener's soul and heart with a sensation of extraordinary well-being in the body. This is why I do what I do, and the way I do. When I compose, it's a feeling, a sound, a vibration, an inspiration from the Angels that comes through my ears and flow instantly through my hands. It is so simple and takes no work, yet it took me a huge amount of work, time and thoughts to understand and accept that. I used to be confronted with a memory that my brain had recorded at the time when my dad told me repeatedly that 'only hard work would pay off'. When I was allowing Spirit to work/play music through me/my hands, it demanded no amount of work, as I was used only as a vessel. Even though my friends and other people were finding this music totally unique and wonderful, I was fighting the education received. "How could this music be great when it took me no work or effort to do it?" The frustration would even be greater when I was creating a piece of music that took me a significant amount of hard work, as I was using my brain this time, and as a result would hear the same people say they thought it was just okay. I guess that the ego could not find any satisfaction through the creation that had required no work.

It took me many long years to understand that the greatest work I could ever do demanded no work and that I only needed to let the Joy of Spirit flow in my heart!

Many have asked in the past "How do you compose your music?" wondering the type of recording studio that I have. Since the age of 19 when I started to compose music for myself, I have learned to use a minimum of equipment. Have you ever heard the saying: less is more? This totally applies to the way I create music. To only have a few key pieces of equipment, but learn to use it all. I learned that from when I was a sound engineer for French television. My boss at the time taught me very useful tips on how to make a great sound out of very little. For instance, while many famous recording studios are impressive to the eye of the producer that will rent this studio for his client (singer), perhaps only 20% of the capacity of the studio will be used. Studios do know that, but they need to add stuff, such as blinking lights in many machines in order to give an illusion of ultra performance and also that you get enough for your money. So I learned to create music with what little I had, and even though now I own three keyboards, I use no gadgets at all. I am sure many of you would be shocked to see what little equipment that I use to produce and create my music. I had a conversation one day with people in Los Angeles who perform live with big rock stars. I was telling them how I create music. They never wanted to believe me. They shared that even when they perform live, and they 'pretend' to the audience that they suddenly jam, having a good time, this was well rehearsed before and that nothing can be spontaneous when you are professional. This of course made me smile a lot internally as for me it is only when I am spontaneous letting Spirit flow in the moment that I create the most beautiful music that will resonate in the listener's heart. When I give an improvised one hour concert by simply allowing the Angels' music to flow through my hands ('The Music of the Soul' explained in more detail in the next chapter) for an entire audience, it is always very powerful, reconnecting everyone in an instant to who they are, I am only using two keyboards and that's it. It is like in everything else. Take cooking for instance, do you need the ultra sophisticated and complicated cook book in order to make a great meal or can you let yourself be inspired by the eyes of your heart? For the music that I create, I only need to listen and feel in order to manifest the Angels' inspired music. It is because it comes from that place of a loving heart that the music may be received as extremely soothing, calming, and for some healing.

The way I have composed all of my albums is quite unique. I start by waiting for the day when the Angels will 'download' the music through me. The process begins with a feeling regarding the theme of the album, then it usually takes many months of waiting for the day when the Angels will start sending the music through me, a bit like a central computer (the Angels) would transfer files to a terminal (me).

I place my hands on my keyboards, close my eyes, and the creation begins. The length of creation for each album varies from one to five days. Add to that, one day for the mix, one day for the mastering in a professional studio, and usually one day of work with the graphic designer.

What remains the same after composing each album is that I need to listen to it again several times in order to learn it and be able to re-play it. It is always a very amusing and unique process for a composer, whom normally is sensed to know what he had done, when using his mind, his brain, writing the music on sheet paper or not. This is why in concert I always prefer to let the Angels improvise through me. The Joy comes from doing something new, playing for the audience that is present. After an album is done, the excitement then becomes what creation will come next.

A radio DJ asked me once "If what you say is true, it must be difficult for you to take credit for something you do not entirely do?" I do take credit for this music, since as a soul, I chose to be of Service to Spirit, the vessel, the antenna on Earth, in which this download would not otherwise take place. The Angels could not download it through me if I did not accept to be of service in the first place, and I could not do what I do without the Angels. It is a total collaboration.

Cousteau's Dream

Just a few months after relocating to Los A
ber 1999, the most beautiful validation of my life purpose a...
gift that the Angels could have sent my way took place the day
when Mr. Terence Yallop, founder of the new age label, Real
Music, located in Sausalito, California called me to ask if I would
accept to be a part of a compilation album in homage to Jacques-
Yves Cousteau to raise money for his Foundation. As I was
French, and one of my instrumental songs 'Future of the Sea'
was mixed with the sounds of whales, the producer asked me to
make a special version solely for the purpose of this album,
which featured me with luminaries such as Yanni, Kenny G,
Vangelis, Kitaro among many others. This CD is great for yoga,
tai chi, massage, relaxation, meditation. I am forever grateful to
Mr. Yallop to having given me this opportunity.

Voyage of the Soul

This is my first solo instrumental album and gathers various
older and newer pieces into an uplifting listening process. This
CD was named from its main quality, to help your soul to travel
anywhere as far as in the galaxies; to feel, remember and re-
awaken to the infinite power within your Self.

Even though it cannot be proved, and I have no intention to
sell this CD as a medical miracle aide, it is fair to mention that
many people have reported signs of significant improvement in
their health status while listening to this album.

Tracks go from very soothing to more upbeat, therefore it is
not your common meditation, relaxation CD. This album is a

listening process that you are invited to follow and accept in order to bring forth its benefits within you.

The album begins with 'Higher Voice' that connects you to the realm of the Angels in an instant. Followed by 'Peace' which is probably one of my favorite tracks on the album, as it opens up your heart chakra, also called center of energy, to its maximum capacity. Knowing that its possibility is endless, as the heart connects to infinite love, it is a piece that is assured to make you feel very well centered. 'Dream within a Dream' is a succession of dreams linked with a musical bridge. It is alive and joyful. You are invited to find the innocence of your inner-child within this song. 'On top of the mountain' was written with the visualization that names the title of this song, such as a yogi man, sitting wisely on top of the mountain to reflect on his life and the world, which leads to the next song that reflects on the 'Future of the Sea'. 'Voyage of the Soul' is a 12 minute track containing the blueprint of this album, followed by 'Beautiful Swan', dedicated to the swans of Bruges' Canals, Belgium, that gave me the inspiration for this piece. A pianistic 'Reflection' followed by 'Promenade', a surprising joyful piece that sees a bagpipe swinging with an orchestra to open doors of your creativity, and your wild imagination. A Greek folk air gently comes to flirt with your soul with 'Agape', leading to 'Inner Serenity', a thoughtful piano song before embracing the 'Full Circle' of this album.

Listened to as background music in the car, this CD also enhances considerably your vision of the scenery into a tri-dimensional living picture.

Soaring with the Angels

This album is one of the most relaxing CDs in my entire collection. The background of the CD cover is a real picture of a magnificent sunset taken from the house where I was living at the time in Desert Hot Springs, California. You can see the portal of lights of the vortex at the entrance of the Coachella Valley. It will calm down any living being, from human to animal. Many use it to calm down their pets and I am even aware of some people using it in their barns to calm down the horses before children ride them. Massage therapists love it!

This is also a great album to just lay back and relax at home after a long busy day. Like the title says, you will soar with the Angels. Since this album is very relaxing, it is not recommended to listen to it while driving, unless you need it to distress from major metropolitan traffic congestion (smile).

The first two instrumental songs are the favorites of many. 'Heaven Sent' invites you to let go of your busy life for a moment to soar with the Angels, which magically creates a 'Moment of Bliss' within. You feel enveloped with the vibration of 'Good Thoughts' and in the Silence of Eternity, you are 'Soaring with the Angels' and hear 'Whistling Grace' chanting you a haunting song for peace. From far above, you hear the sounds of the Ocean, which you connect to by sending a 'Celestial Lullaby' melody. The Ocean responds to you and invites you to a 'Pursuit of Dreams' where you are invited to fly over the Ocean at a fast pace and feel the freedom invade your entire being. After this course, the Cherubs will take you for a ballad, and show you that 'You Have the Face of An Angel', before you surrender entirely to the 'Ethereal Glory'. You know your message have been received when you hear, coming from earth, the sounds of someone playing the 'Celestial Lullaby' that you sang earlier.

This feeling is immense and you are embraced by the bliss in the 'Stillness of the Aurora'.

Dolphins… A Message of Love

I had in mind to release what could be the album 'Reflection'. However no inspiration was coming thru which is often a sign this was not the right time for it. I accepted that I had to put this one on hold.

One day, I literally felt the spirit of the dolphins ask me if I would accept them to download their music to me, as a 'calling to spread the consciousness of infinite pure love to the world.' I was used to hearing the Angels communicate with me but this was the first for me to hear the dolphins' Spirit. As soon as I said yes, two days later, the dolphins started to share with me, on a spiritual level, our direct connection with them. Their message may shock some of you that are protectors of the dolphins, as it had shocked me too at first, but I am only reporting what I heard directly from them. They shared that some of them had accepted to be abducted solely for the purpose of humans' entertainment/education and that their sacrifice was worth it when they participated in shifting the consciousness of a child or an adult by just the fact they had a close encounter with them, such as swimming together. These encounters can be life changing and very healing for children with challenges, such as autism, etc.

They also shared about our ancient spiritual connection, that we used to live together long, long ago, and there came a time when the earth was not to be free anymore. The dolphins chose to go to the Ocean to keep their freedom, whereas humans chose to stay on land, with only the illusion of freedom. They said this is why they will always consider humans as their friends by coming to say 'hello', swimming near their boats. They do not want to live through fear by wondering if this boat will bring them harm or not. They say "It is the price we pay to keep our Spirits free and to not disconnect with who we are." They say that dolphins have a direct connection from the greatest depths of the Ocean to the farthest galaxies. Those that we see in the Seas and Oceans are only a link between both worlds.

They seemed very pleased that I accepted their request for this album to be made. They asked me to go buy a new keyboard. I was already living in the desert at the time, and went to Los Angeles for this purchase. At the store, I asked a sales assistant to turn all the keyboards on, so I can try them. The dolphins had assured me that I would know which one to buy. After trying all of them, I was left void; when suddenly the sales person told me that they had just received a new one that was not hooked up yet. Once hooked up, he showed me briefly how to use it and left me to play with it. My hands, trembling from excitement, touched several buttons at once when suddenly appeared a pre-selected sound called DOLPHIN RIDE. My eyes opened wide, I started to play and all the people in the store turned back saying "What is that?" with an astonished tone in their voices? I understood quickly that it was the sign the dolphins had talked about and I purchased this instrument on the spot.

One afternoon, I was practicing on this keyboard when suddenly came a powerful piece of music through my hands. When I finished, I stood up and cried non-stop for about 15-20 minutes as this music had embraced me with overflowing pure love. The only problem is that I had not recorded it. A friend of mine suggested me to call the Dolphins' Spirit again and ask them to send me the music again, which took place two hours later. The title of the album: A MESSAGE OF LOVE, track #5 on the album was born. All of the other songs came together very quickly and the entire CD was completed in only 3 days.

'Welcome' embraces you in the Kingdom of The Infinite Love, where the dolphins live in their spirit, what they represent and who they are. Like a 'Ballet of Light', their love gently flows to your enchantment. 'Waves of Love' emanates from your heart, which establishes a 'Sincere Communion' with the Dolphins. 'A Message of Love' enraptures you, while Virgin 'Marie de la Mer' (Mary of the Sea) gracefully enchants you. This is a true 'Revelation' for you, and a time to digest the sparkles of the glorious music coming from the most beautiful place in the galaxies, from the core essence of the heart, the heart of the Universe. This brings you 'Calm in your Spirit', before splashing waves of Joy. You can then say "From my Heart" to you, "Angels of the Sea", I highly salute you with the most gracious "Reverence", an infinite 'Dance of Love' to "Rejoice" of your Presence, to honor you, to embrace you in the infinity of our deepest connection.

When I compose music, it is very often accompanied with visuals, like a music video. Here is a beautiful story about track #11, 'Angels of the Sea', that will help you better understand and to feel it with a totally different dimension. I was on the beach when dolphins came to see me. They asked me not to be afraid, and to go with them beneath the Ocean. For a moment I thought this was not possible as I was going to drown but they reassured me that I would be just fine in their company. I put my hands on their dorsal fins and they took me gently into the Ocean and surrounded me. As they started to speed, I found myself floating on the water with their heavenly presence on each side. It was a great feeling. After a while they told me we were going to dive in, which we did in an instant. We were going deeper and deeper and deeper. "Deep enough where humans cannot find

THE POWER OF SOOTHING MUSIC

us here", they said. Then there appeared a strange bright blue light mixed with a bright light out of a dark hole, like a cave, a tunnel, an entrance to another world beneath the Ocean, the 'Treasures of Humanity.' It felt like the Great Central Sun, the Source of All Sources. I was not allowed to go inside, but I could perceive strange life creatures that I had never seen before. Dolphins said that they were living and hiding here, as there were not yet given permission to show themselves to human life. Then they brought me back to shore.

This album embraces you with unconditional Love. It is a great album to listen to for women who are in the stages of pregnancy, as the baby will love to feel the vibration of the dolphins and the water. Babies love this album. It is a great CD for anyone to listen to on a daily basis, as it recalls your direct spiritual connection with the dolphins, therefore it recollects and reconnects you with who you truly are, the beautiful soul that you are, living a human experience. Enjoy!

Symphony of Light

This album is dedicated to 'the Angel on the Mountain' in Palm Springs, California, and was composed from my home, which at the time had a direct view of this angelic phenomenon. This album was made in Her Honor and took 4 days to complete.

One day, while mixing the album, I went to the patio of my house, looked at the 'Angel on the Mountain' and suddenly had a vision of seeing the image of Christ. I shook my head, closed my eyes and looked again. It was still there. I took a photograph of it, to make sure it was not illusive, and it was there.

Both 'The Angel' and 'The Christ' etched in the San Jacinto Mountain, in Palm Springs, California. I was in awe.

The process of this album was just amazing. It felt like many Classical Composers came from Heaven to jam with me on the Earth, and with the intervention of the Angels I could capture their Joy, their Happiness, their Freedom, and their Serenity. With all humility, it felt like the Great Composers came to play with me.

The album begins with a multitude of musical sparkles with a vocal choir for a glorious 'Heart Illumination', in which you can let yourself go to surrender to the 'Beauty of Forgiveness" from a variation of 'Fur Elise' by Beethoven. Forgiveness accomplished, you are free to fly over Palm Springs with this charming and enchanting ballad 'Flying over the Canyons', from the right side of the canyons, crossing over the Canyons to the left side, you are flying free and letting yourself transport to the secret of this place. You land where and when you can hear the 'Sounds of Intensity' revealed by this haunting valley. Flowers blooming everywhere, you are overwhelmed by such 'Scents of Joy', this Tchaikovsky-like dance that perfumes your soul with happy incantation. In the sky, you look and see a 'Rainbow of Flowers' appear for your pure enjoyment. This valley reveals to you the power of its Native American name 'In the palm of God's Hand' with this variation of 'Ode of Joy' by Beethoven and be blessed kneeling to its empowering majesty. Sit near the abundant stream coming from the snow melting and appreciate this delightful song, before hearing the bells of the Light, resonating in the entire Valley and Canyons. Start flying while surrendering to the captivating power of this 'Symphony of Light'. A Strauss-like 'Concert from Heaven' can be heard, which allows the magnificent 'Colors of Harmony' to blossom. It is a calm 'Morning at the Spring' where the birds you hear and the sounds of the stream on the rocks are rejuvenating, heartfelt and light spirited. 'The Angel on the Mountain' sings a song to your heart, which prepares you to embrace the spirit of 'The Emotion of Love'.

I have a little anecdote in regards to this latest song. My ears from early age were able to hear the most subtle sound and I battled with the fact of being too much of a perfectionist. This track was very important to me in the process of releasing it. After I composed this song in about 15 minutes; the real-time length of the piece for the piano, and the second layer for the violins, I realized that there were some false notes at one place, and it was difficult to let go. However I learned in the past that retouching a piece through a computerized system, gave it less intensity, less power. It was essential for me not to worry about the false notes my hands could provoke while playing and focus more on what is important; the energetic power of the music at the time it comes through! The imperfections, then becomes the seductive perfection. Is it a coincidence why most people consider this particular their favorite from the entire album?

Reflection

This album is dedicated to one of my favorite Sand dunes in California. The first time I discovered these sand dunes filled my soul with such joy that it is difficult to describe with words.

The story behind the design of the CD cover is a perfect example of what happens when you connect to the eyes of your heart. While David, the graphic designer, and I were working on this cover trying to fit a picture of me walking down the sand dunes that some dear friends had taken of me for the occasion, we were experiencing some difficulties to center the picture. We decided to crop the picture but then realized it was not filling up the page and we were missing some blue sky. David is a very inspired man and allows the Angels to work through him to facilitate the process of the design and was guided to copy the picture and turn it upside down in order for the two blue skies to coincide. He had no idea that this little trick would create the cover of the album. By sliding the picture down suddenly appeared the top of the sand dunes upside down and by a guided mistake, he slid the picture too much when suddenly we had the magical goose bumps that tell us of the validation of the truth. By letting the eyes of our hearts blindly guide us, the cover was made. Viewed from the side, there appears an hour glass of time related to reflection.

When I arrived in the Coachella Valley, I first visited the touristic places around here, and learned that a long time ago there were a lot of sand dunes out here. However with the population growing in this valley, and the many golf courses being built, covered the sand with grass, and the sand dunes became a rare thing to witness. I went to a store specializing in detailed maps for hikers, etc and asked them for the closest sand dunes, as my intuition was telling me there was one left nearby. Nobody knew until someone mentioned the large sand dunes in the San Luis Obispo area, north of Santa Barbara along the shore. I smiled at them nicely, thanked them for their time, and picked up on the spot, two books that had jumped to mind after catching my eye. When I opened one of the books, the pictures I saw invaded my spirit with such enthusiasm, that I drove there right away. Driving my car just before Sunset on a road in the middle of sand dunes overwhelmed me. After walking on the dunes for some time, I saw someone in front of me. He was a nice tall man dressed in a long white robe, with a white turban on his head to protect himself from the sun and possibly a sand storm. It made me feel so happy and whole, as this man was just a reflection of me in a past life. Every time I go to this magical place, this phenomenon occurs and pours into the core essence of my entire being. It is a spiritual, emotional, physical, an intense well-being, recollection, and reconnection of my soul.

When you read the sentence on the CD: "I invite you to reflect on the events in your life and surrender them to peace & love and bring forgiveness to yourself and anyone involved," you will now know what it refers to.

Also, when I walk on these dunes, I feel so blessed to be able to feel the blueprint of the dolphins and whales that had once swum here a long time ago when this part of the world was still an Ocean. Once I even saw a large dune reflecting the shape of a dolphin. This is why this album is called "Reflection".

The music for this album was composed in 1 single day and talks to your soul. It is great for deep relaxation, and massage. It is also perfect to play in the background when you have precious guests for a nice dinner at home.
Track #10 has a Middle Eastern flair, in homage to the reflection of my past life. The titles of the eleven tracks form a poem:

"I feel
the sensual touch on the sand
beneath the footprints of my sole.

Rays of Light
caress my Spirit
with tender Passion.

Beyond Eternity
I remember
the Power of Silence

Through the immensity of my heart
I am Free."

This album is very personal and reflects well who I am as a soul living in this current human experience.

A Mind like an Ocean

This CD is the completion of a series of inspired synchronized events. I had the title of the album for a long time but the inspiration for the music was still in the ether. One day I thought of creating a festival about Angels and Dolphins, but after many thoughts, started to think that perhaps I should drop the dolphins and make it a Festival about Angels only, as most might wonder how the dolphins have anything to do with Angels. The phone rang and Eva Sakmar-Sullivan was calling me to tell me how much she enjoyed my "Dolphins... A Message of Love" CD that she listened to while painting. As soon as she had said that, I knew that the Angels had guided her to call me, right after having my doubts, so I would again include the Dolphins in the Festival. During the conversation she gave me the name of her website and when I later checked it out, my eyes felt immediate admiration. A rare purity of art that felt very familiar. I called her again and during the conversation, my voice suddenly said, before thinking "It would be just wonderful to have paintings like that on a CD cover." She immediately replied that she would and when I shared the title of my next CD "A Mind Like an Ocean" she got the chills. She said she would work on it without condition. It was a pure angelic loving connection.

At the same time, the musical inspiration was still not there. Eva finally called saying that the painting was finished and she could hear the music of the next album being of very high vibration, even higher than the previous albums. She had created this masterpiece while listening to the Dolphins album. Still no inspiration was coming through. Finally one day, I heard the Angels say that I should call Eva to ask her to purchase the original painting. I called her and she sweetly accepted. The day I received it, I felt as if I was transported inside of the painting and alive in it. I knew the Angels had asked me to purchase it to get the inspiration. During the next 4 days, I composed this album with the original artwork in front of me. It was like a movie being lived in real time, which you can feel when you listen to it, similar to a movie soundtrack.

This CD opens doors, those of your unknown gifts, and any other.

'A Mind Like an Ocean'. The timbales resonate, captivate your attention, and initiate to let the Power of the Light of the Ocean wash your negative thoughts and busy mind. 'The Journey Begins.' The sounds of the waves gently caress the most persisting tensions, trust and 'Believe' in the joyfulness and lightness of your inner power and in the liberation you will be feeling after completion of this voyage. Your soul remembers that living 'In the Breath of Life' is the only way to deliverance. Let flow the multitude of inspired guidance that your 'Intuition' is sending you, soul travel through the calm forcefulness and feel the intensity of your deepest 'Inspiration' until you can cheerfully dance the 'Celebration' of your personal and spiritual achievement. Acknowledge and rejoice with a 'Prayer Dance' and 'With a Gentle Heart.' Take a moment to recollect and reconnect your entire being. Feel the power of 'A New Life' emerging to you. Doors are opening up to you with infinite possibilities; bless them with a heartfelt touch of 'Gratitude.'

> *"Let the Power of the Light of the Ocean*
> *wash your negative thoughts and busy mind*
> *so you can re-enter feeling free in your own Kingdom...*
> *The one of your own Heart!"*

Eyes of your Heart

This solo instrumental musical album is considered "The Music of The Soul' of the book's title and invites you to find the clarity of your own truth. It allows you to feel and create a luminous perspective of your own life by opening the doors of awareness and seeing through the eyes of your heart.

The story behind this CD cover also deserves to be told. I wrote the entire book with an Angelite sphere (healing stone from Peru) in front of me, between the keyboard and the screen of my computer, as shown in the illustration of Chapter Nineteen. Spirit had guided me to take photographs of a red cloth that I had, as well as the Angelite sphere. When I met with David, the graphic designer, I showed him a picture of my Angel lover dog that passed away twenty three years ago and he asked me to connect to 'Tatane'. Right away his spirit was in the room and as an Angel he placed himself behind David, the same way Angels stand behind me when I create music. Suddenly David started to draw inspired movements and objects on a piece of paper. He then took a photograph of a cloth I had taken. You have to know I had taken dozens of pictures with the same material but without even looking at all of them, David chose one and started to place it in his template. He then placed the Angelite sphere on top of that and after a while we had the famous goose bumps of the validation of the truth when we saw that the wrinkles of the cloth formed the shape of a pyramid with the Angelite at the top. More amazing, when I took the picture of the sphere with a flash, it had the light of the flash in the middle of the sphere and that light came at the top of the pyramid, exactly like what David had drawn without really knowing what he was doing, while 'Tatane' was working through him. Perhaps for some of you, you may think this is way too much of a story, but believe me, this is nothing but the truth and this is exactly how it unfolded. The picture of a Greek statue in the middle of the Angelite sphere was also taken 23 years ago at the time I was living in an apartment in Paris, France. We were hesitating to either place my dog's face or the statue on the cover. It was then that 'Tatane' told me that he was there and his spirit was in the book, and he did not feel the need to be in the book as he had no ego where he was and he laughed out loud. The amusing thing is that 'Tatane' who died 23 years ago guided us to place the image of that statue that I had also taken 23 years ago. It is his way to be on the cover of the book without appearing physically.

David and I always have stories like this each time we work together. It is a blessing working with someone who allows himself to see through the eyes of his heart.

I highly encourage you to take the time each day, to listen to the source of your inspirations, to listen to the guidance of your Heart when it sparkles with pure and joyful lights, to listen to what empowers your Soul, and to honor all of them by taking the appropriate action so you can merge with all of them to live in the wholeness of the Being that you chose to be.

Life
Lovingly
Breathe it in
Dance it sincerely
Sing your song joyfully
Exhale the rapture all around
Listen to every sound and vibration
As a blessed Soul living a human experience

CHAPTER SIXTEEN

THE MUSIC OF THE SOUL

As mentioned in Chapter Four, a few months after my N.D.E, I felt guided to play the name of a French singer that I had just watched on TV. After repeatedly playing it for about 7 minutes, I suddenly felt as if I was peeking through a multi dimensional window in the Universe where I was able to clearly perceive, feel and hear her distress, her call for help, her true feelings, which were drastically different from her televised appearance. This shocked and also scared me as I did not understand exactly what had happened and whether I may have violated a Universal Law. What did I know about the Universal Law at the age of 13? That is however what I had said to myself.

Without knowing it, I had experienced for the very first time, what would become my most important God given musical gift. A gift that is so natural, so simple, yet took me so long to fully accept. Could it be that our most desired answers may just be unfolding in front of our eyes, so simply, and effortless that we don't see it, for we long to take a more confusing and complex detour to prove to ourselves that we can cross the challenges and therefore that we are worth something?

God gave me a gift that seems to combine the knowledge and experience of several past lives; the massage, the healing, the music and the devotion to Spirit, and the validation was given to me during an Aura reading/painting I had in my early 30's. However this is only when I relocated to the USA that I felt totally comfortable to express and share this gift with others. The first time I shared my gift was at a metaphysical bookstore in West Hollywood, California where I had rented the room for a lecture with a live demonstration. The Angels always chose who come on stage. I close my eyes and let them describe details of the person they chose. It can be as simple as "Who in this audience had a cat that passed away that you used to dress with pinkish clothing?" or "Who is named Mario?" or "Who has a mother that just passed away who was a professional dancer?" etc.

A woman was called on stage who did not like her birth name because of an issue with her dad. She had associated her last name with who she was, so she changed her name totally. She sat facing the audience so people would be able to witness the before, during and after effect the music of her soul had on her. She felt a little uncomfortable and mostly skeptical about the entire concept, wondering how simply listening to her 'own music' channeled through me could change it all. However she was brave and had faith in God to accept to come on stage in front of an entire audience and be used for this demonstration. Her Higher Self probably knew of the benefits she would receive but her ego was doubting and skeptical. The Angels had their reasons for choosing her – to help her but also for others to relate to her struggle, which consequently would help them to heal as well. When the first musical notes of her full birth name began to play through my hands, she took a tissue as she was starting to sob. Her reaction was immediate and lasted for the next 10 to 15 minutes until the music stopped. The audience was speechless and you could have heard a fly in the silence of the full house. I went by her side, and asked her if she was willing to share the experience. She said while trembling with overwhelming deep joy that it took her only a few seconds to reconcile with her true name. She was sorry that she detached from it for the wrong reasons, and that she would go back to it from now on. She also added that she had forgotten how beautiful her name was and felt whole again after this reconciliation. It was moving, and astonishing to see how fast it took her to get it, and to heal from it. Her face was rejoicing for making peace with who she is. She had run away from her own vibrations, from who she originally was and wearing someone else's responsibility on her shoulder. Now she was set free and it was awesome for everyone to witness.

Let me explain what had just occurred, from what the Angels have taught me. The Angels always say that the name that we receive at birth is divinely guided, and contains the energetic vibrations and frequencies to help us achieve our life purpose, mission, and to live a balanced and connected life. Creating a catchier name as an artist or someone in show business is fine to do for the purpose of marketing as long as you remain at peace with your full name given to you at birth. However, changing your name because you associated, identified, or defined who you are with any member of your family that may have caused you abuse or trauma and who also carries the same name may become a real issue to you, as you co-created to live an illusion-ary life that is not yours. By consequence, your new name may modify the vibrations and energy of the life purpose, mission, and therefore your destiny. You now live a life that is not yours, which will bring forth confusion, fights, battles within, and po-tential physical blockages that will manifest as either, barriers in the achieving your goals, or physically within your body.

When the lady we talked about earlier at the music of the soul demonstration reconciled with her divinely guided name, her full name given to her at her birth, she sobbed from her new-found understanding that she had been defining herself, and carrying someone else's baggage and responsibility. This aware-ness cleared up the trauma in an instant and she was able to let go of the person's identity and reconnect with her True Self, set-ting her free. This is just an example of freedom, reconnection, and recollection that is received when I play 'The Music of Your Soul™.'

In our Society we can change names, add nicknames as often and as we want, without being aware of the heavy consequences it may have on us. How many people are currently living a life that is not their own? Let's take an example of a man coming for a session, complaining that his life was so messed up and he could not understand why. He prayed to the Angels and God, but like he said, it seemed like they were busy somewhere else and they never listened to him or gave him any answers.

If this is happening to you too, you want to ask yourself?

* Am I truly living my own life? This refers to the life that you had chosen to live as a soul living this human experi-ence.

* Am I defining my life to my job, my car, my success, my wealth?

* Am I defining myself as being me, breathing and loving the musical vibrations of the name that I carry for the sole purpose of my mission in this lifetime?

Which of these applies to you?

Please remember who you are, the powerful being that you are, who has infinite powers. Don't fall in the trap of being the victim of your own creation! Many times, I see people who think they have been the victims of magical stuff, etc, while in reality they were just the victims of their own self creations. Their egos would make them believe to blame others, for not having to face their responsibility to forgive, and love uncondi-tionally. In most cases, when we live disconnected from all, we become the creator of our own self destruction.

The Music of the Soul™, Personalized CD

I would like to take a moment now to describe what this CD really is.

The Music of the Soul™ is a personalized CD based on the musical vibrations of your full name given to you at birth. A CD can be created for one individual, a couple, a group, a company, and in this case, a book's name and purpose.

You can find the CD: Eyes of Your Heart available at:
www.FredericDelarue.com.

When giving me your full name, you give me permission to connect with you at a soul level, with the help of the Angels. We have talked earlier about people changing names but 'The Music of Your Soul™' is not just about names; it is essentially to help you to reconnect to the power of who you truly are, while listening to your own music. When you feel disconnected, out of your shoes like many of us would say, confused, stressed, and lonely, listening to your own music is like breathing and bathing in the energetic river of vibrations of who you truly are, of your beautiful soul and of your own power which may bring forth an instant haven of peace, a recollection of positive thoughts, a reconnection to your own Self. This bliss occurs when you allow yourself to be in the center of the music. It is like your private dance of rejuvenation. Allow your body cells to breathe in your own healthy vibration, the one you came on earth with, the original one that was still pure before finding itself swayed by the struggles of human life. Let the music flow in your blood while warmly and gently enveloping the energy field of your own musical Light. Practice the Law of Attraction by sending your love to the Universe, to the Angels, to God, and feel the power of yours coming back instantly. It is a personal and intimate moment with your Self.

For a united couple, it is all the above, amplified by the fact that you will have a better understanding, awareness, and clarity of the higher purpose of your union, the reasons for your connection, and what and who you truly are and mean to each other. It is the ultimate bonding experience of two souls accepting to grow, evolve and glow together. For a couple experiencing some issues, but are willing to work on them together, listening to your music can benefit you both ways. In the event you were together with your partner for the wrong reasons (many still confuse true love with sexual, physical attachment), you might receive clearly the message that you had nothing to do together and might choose to separate with peace in order to find a soul whom you can bond with, on all levels. In the event you are with the right partner for you, but experienced mostly little ego-based issues (I call them 'little' because in reality they are so insignificant, but if you let these ego-based issues become a major part of your life's decisions, it may become a huge illusionary problem), the outcome of listening to your music together may be overwhelmingly life-changing, as you may feel who you are to one another, in the deepest of your heart and soul. Your little issues then dissipate in an instant and you are able to laugh about them, seeing the bigger and clearer picture of your union.

For a company, a spa, a healing center, a specialty store, or a shopping center to have 'The Music of Your Soul™' made on demand is great when you want your clientele to be nicely welcomed, and enveloped within the higher purpose of your mission statement. This may ultimately generate more business as the energy is flowing effortlessly.

The music is simultaneously recorded on a CD, printed under your birth name(s), or the name of your company, spa, church, book, and so on. The CD varies in length, usually about 40 minutes for individuals to 55 minutes for couples. The CD is a series of musical sequences, varying from ethereal sounds to piano, from low sounds to those that are high pitched and is a natural process to healing, whatever it may be for you, from emotional traumas, to wounds from the past, to physical healing. The low sounds are not to be mistaken for sadness, but for going deeper within the depth of your soul. They naturally find the source of the causes of traumas and release them gently. All you need to do is to fully accept and breathe them in. The higher pitches help you to reconnect to the Angelic Realm. All you need to do is to be as open as you can be, and let the music gently flow within your soul, your mind, and all the cells of your body. The Angels guide me to create this music for you, for your benefit, and they know what they are doing. They know exactly which music played will help you in your journey.

Many people ask how I knew it was their music if there were several people with the same name. To that, I can answer that Angels know who the intention is focused on as they guide my hands, they know which notes, and how to play those notes, how long to stay on a particular note, to trigger a negative or painful vibration of the past to be released gently out of your energy field. It is almost for sure that there is at least someone on this earth that has the same name as you. However it is 'The Music of Your Soul!' Your soul is unique and there is only one like you. Even though we may be all connected one to another, we are all unique in this collectiveness. So there is no worry to have whether I play your music or someone else's.
There is no confusion possible and I invite you to read the many testimonials received that are listed on my website at: www.FredericDelarue.com.

Many times I am asked how I was able to know which music was theirs. The answer to that is: I don't, it is the Angels that know. I am just the vessel through which it flows. Many people have reported that they have already heard some of the music played during a Near Death Experience they had. Like I said, the Angels know. Each CD is totally unique with a specific melody. There is absolutely no identical CD. Even if sometimes the format is similar as the process for healing may be similar, the music is always unique to your soul.

This personalized CD reflects your soul's mission, and who you truly are. It is a wonderful experience to connect to your Self in this way, and on such a high level, that you may have never have done before. To meditate and listen to your music, make sure you either sit or lay comfortably, take three deep breaths in order to send out to God or the Angels all of your worries with total trust and faith, and be in the silence of your own power to listen to who you truly are at a soul level. Accept whatever is being revealed to you without holding any judgment. Moments of your life may come up to the surface while listening to your own music, even those which were painful to you. Watch these moments as they unfold, as if you are in a movie theater, or watching television, with no emotional attachment. Watch the role of the lead actress or actor (you) with the same detachment; and when what described above has been honored properly, the music will do its job with a gentle expression and manner to release it for good from your energy field. While listening to your own music, focus on the power of the silence within, feel your body, your breathing, your heartbeat, your Higher Self (for most about six inches above your crown chakra), your Soul, your inner child (in the area of your heart). Only through the complete Silence, you may receive your deepest and most meaningful blessings. The Angels usually say that it takes only one second for them to bless you. One second is necessary to surrender totally. We will develop this in a later Chapter about the Healing Angels.

When I look back at my life, I realize that I fought for 17 years fearing the extreme power of this unique method. For the 13 year old child that I was, it was a little bit much to digest and to fully comprehend.

As I conclude this chapter, I would like to restate the most important lesson. Before thinking of changing your name, think it over and make sure that the reason is not to disconnect to a last name that reminds you of a traumatic incident or person. You want to make sure to live your own life and not someone else's. The way to do this is to stay in harmony with the music of your soul, which is your name given to you at birth.

CHAPTER SEVENTEEN

Ego Tricks

The ego is a complex subject that cannot be detailed in its entirety here. Many authors have already written about it if you are interested to delve further into the subject. However as part of my own experiences, I wish to briefly demonstrate the use of our ego, and also its tricks.

The ego is an entity which is part of us. We have to learn to coexist with it.

When the reflection that others project towards you is good, or positive, such as: you are so cute, you are so intelligent, you are the best, you are great, you are a genius, you, you, you, it builds up your ego tremendously. The trick is, as it usually feels very good to be flattered, that you might identify your Self with your ego. For example, if I ask you, who are you, what will be your answer? If you answered "I am a doctor", or if you feel the need to claim your PhD or Dr. to everyone and all the time, this indicates that you are identifying your Self as your ego, in other word, you define yourself being your ego. In other words, you define yourself being your ego. This is the trick most of us fall into, and this terrible disease of our Society triggers most cases of depression!

If you find yourself facing a competitive battle with your colleagues or facing depression because of the stress at work, and so forth, in most cases it is that you define your job as being you. This is another ego trick. You are not your job and never will be. You are you. When you define yourself with your job, with the car you drive, with the home you live in, with the jewelry or clothing you wear, etc you bring the greatest smile to the huge pharmaceutical industry as depression tickles you.

When the reflection that others project towards you is judgmental, such as: you are a stupid, you are ugly, you are awful, you are fat, you are lousy, etc., it can tear you apart if you allow yourself to identify your Self as such and begin to feel unworthy, your ego has played the trick once more against you.

If you were living alone on a deserted island, with no other human beings around, your ego would not be as developed because there would be no mirror it could reflect onto, no people to admire and flatter you, or conversely, cut your down.

So what do we do in order to live with the ego, use it when needed, without falling victim to its tricks? The ego can be used to appreciate things, without referring to those things as part of who you are. One great example in our modern and plastic Society is the major impact that the media and magazines have on our egos. They tell you how you ought to look, what you need to wear, how you need to smell, and what you need to say. Those of you following these models may end up identifying yourselves through the reflection of these models. So when someone tells you "Wow you look fashionable today!" or "You are a genius!" your ego might enjoy a delusional orgasm in response to being flattered, and the trick is that you might define yourself as that, instead of the soul that you truly are. The trick is when you start enjoying that, you are on a very rough road as the ego will always play tricks on you, to confuse you with who you are. Therefore you are on the edge of not living YOUR life but the life of your ego.

Take the example in Chapter Fourteen when you were invited to visualize your Self flying above your body from different angles above the room, similar to a video camera in each corner of the ceiling in the room watching and observing your behaviors. If you had an angry attitude, and you learn to detach yourself from your egoistic point of view, and observe yourself from the virtual video cameras in the corners of your room, what would you see? What would you do? How would you feel? Most likely, you would feel sorry for that person down below that feels so much in disarray, and after some time, you might just laugh out loud at how silly this whole situation looks. What is important is for you to be aware of what the ego makes you do, or think, or behave! Once you have awareness of its tricks, its power dissipates and you can laugh at the situation.

Why do you think marketing and sales people are told to use the ego-fix? Do you think they really care when they say that you look beautiful today or that they like your outfit? Of course not! They are just flattering your ego, because they know that once your ego has been fed nicely, you feel good, relaxed and ready to listen to them, and you fall victim to their hypnotic mercy. Imagine one moment someone telling you that you are just wonderful because you are a famous actor or lawyer. Do you think your ego will like that? I bet it will love it! Now imagine someone telling you how wonderful you are because you are spiritual. Do you think your ego will like that? I bet it will not care one second. Why? Because it is not attached to the material, nor the physical world! And the ego gets its food mostly from the reflection you received from people's judgments about you, and as judgments are part of the egoistic nature, it never ends. The ego feels powered up when it feels flattered. Authoritarians have a huge ego because they feel they are right all the time, and that they know better than others about everything.

If you know that you are beautiful because you are a child of God, this is different. You know it within your heart. It is real. It is the truth, as it is the core essence of who your beautiful soul is! The ego cannot be fed with spiritual truth, that's the reason why our Society prefers to invade your thoughts with material stuff, because this is the joy of the ego.

Instead of judging others, we could use our differences to help each other evolve, grow and glow. Once we think that we are right, our ego rules the way and dissipates our discernment, peace and love. The ego fights to believe he is right! When you become passionate towards somebody that you don't like, why wouldn't you see him/her as a soul that has been sent to you by God to show you to make peace with a part of yourself that you obviously can see through the other, and refuse to accept? Since it is a horrible job for the ego to work on itself, you, defining yourself as your ego, prefer to judge which brings forth the greatest illusion to feel good.

I consider the ego as a spoiled child who always wants new toys. Once you give him what he wants, he does not care anymore for his toys, he just wants new ones, and so forth. The ego has never enough, and always wants and needs more. The ego is not who you are, it is only a part of you. When you identify yourself with all the things that the ego wants or gets flattered by, it takes all the clarity away from you, and therefore you find yourself more confused about everything because you are not living YOUR life but that of your ego's life. Your eyes may see a pretty dress in which you might look so beautiful wearing. Don't let your ego fool you by thinking you are beautiful thanks to the materialistic appearance of that dress. You are beautiful because of who you are, what you do to be nice to people around you, what you do to make a difference in the world, what you do to contribute to a peaceful environment around you, what you to do keep your planet clean, your respect of nature, etc.

Learn to discern when your ego arrives galloping in and when you surprise yourself being fooled by it, just laugh out loud at the situation.

By being in the Silence of your true self that resides within the eyes of your heart, you will always have clarity.

CHAPTER EIGHTEEN

THE TWIST OF DON'TS

I am certain that you will find a lot of Don'ts in this book just like in any other literature, newspapers, media articles, etc. Don'ts have been part of our daily living for a very long time.

When I first arrived to the United States, I remember wondering why there were so many warning signs such as 'Don't go beyond this point', 'Don't do this', 'Don't do that', 'Don't go there', 'Don't walk around the lake'. There is a 'Don't' for almost anything, in a Nation that is renown for its freedom. Is freedom then limited to what we are allowed to do?

We may confine our cows within a fenced pasture, just to make sure they will not go anywhere beyond the limits of the fences. At first, it appears like they are not free, right? However, on the other hand, they are free to go anywhere they want, to breathe, to eat, to watch the train pass, or to walk or sleep within their own limited enclave. Does that ring a bell to you? Do you find any similarity with our freedom and the limits established within the laws of each country?

Usually, telling someone 'Don't do this' will naturally intrigue their curiosity and they will want to do this forbidden act to find out why it is not allowed. They ask themselves "Why I am not allowed to do this? I want to know what it is like so I will do it just to find out." Have you never been caught doing something you were told not to do? I am certain that we may all have done it, at least once in our life. Like the child that is told not to play with matches, not to steal a cookie out of the cookie jar, not to run into the street, not to play with the TV remote control. What do children do? All of the above!

California has forbidden the use of hand held cell phones while driving quite for some time now. The other day, I was driving peacefully for many hours on the freeway and was focusing on the beautiful landscapes. Suddenly I saw a huge billboard saying "DON'T TEXT AND DRIVE!" What did it provoke in me? Well, besides stopping my focus on watching the scenery, it triggered the thought to look at my cell phone. I had not thought of it before, but the billboard saying not to use cell phones triggered my focus on doing exactly what it told me NOT to do.

If you tell a child to stay in a house and do whatever he wants to do, but ask him not to go to a particular room. What do you think will happen? He may have never thought of it, but because you mentioned it, it triggered his curiosity why he should not go there, and he will probably end up opening the door to that room.

If, from a quiet composer, I was using the power of Don'ts, what would happen?

Imagine a TV Commercial focusing on:

First image:

CAUTION!!!
DON'T LISTEN TO FREDERIC DELARUE'S MUSIC!

Second image:

DON'T LISTEN TO FREDERIC DELARUE'S MUSIC!

Third image:

DON'T LISTEN TO FREDERIC DELARUE'S MUSIC!

Fourth image:

IT COULD CHANGE YOUR LIFE!
www.FredericDelarue.com

What reaction would that commercial provoke in you?

For many, it would trigger their curiosity and they would hurry to the website to see why they shouldn't listen to the music.

Has anyone ever told you "Don't tell this to anybody, you are the only person to know and I trust you"? Some of us will honor the wish, but many others may fall into the following category. The news is so exciting, and the fact of knowing that it should not be repeated, since it is a secret, automatically triggers automatically the itch to tell someone about it, so they do. It is anchored in our brain that 'Don't' must be a very exciting to do, since it is forbidden.

I kept this chapter brief, as I just wanted to give you a glimpse of how we could all learn to use our language and words differently and more effectively to achieve the desired result rather than the opposite.

CHAPTER NINETEEN

THE ALTAR

An altar is a place to reconnect, recharge and find oneself through the collectiveness of energy in the solitude of silence. An altar can be physical, at home, in nature or virtual, through the visualization of your thought.

The most common form of Altar:

For those of you who worship with the help of altars, you may have one at home on a table where you have displayed all of your religious and spiritual items of your belief, candles, incenses, crystals, statues, pictures, etc.

A Natural Altar:

You may also find natural altars in Nature. In the surroundings of Palm Springs, for example, there is a place I love to go, where several oases grew in the middle of the desert, thanks to the San Andreas Fault. The underground water that comes to an abrupt stop along the way by the Fault is forced to resurface bringing up salt, which gives the natural source for palm trees to grow, and the oasis to emerge in the middle of the desert. In one of my other favorite places, where I love to bring people during tours, you have the privilege to experience two oases at once. Standing on the first one feels like being on a Hollywood movie set, and passing through this untouched-by-mankind jungle is quite indescribable. You have to be there to feel and breathe the intensity of the moment. You then arrive to another oasis with a pond that sees more and more water as the Fault keeps releasing more each day, before arriving to your destination; a group of palm trees that I refer to as: 'The Cathedral of Palm Trees.' This is THE perfect natural Altar! You may imagine the chapel on your left, and the main Cathedral right in front of you, assisted by a bench for you to rest, meditate, pray and connect to the Higher Source of oneself. These trees are wonderful teachers of Peace. During the time I was composing the album, Symphony of Light, I would lay on this bench on a very quiet and calm day without any wind. I asked the trees whether they would allow me to take a picture of them to insert in the CD booklet of the album. The answer was immediate as a gentle breeze moved all the leaves on the top of the trees and the intuition of the moment took it for a 'yes'. Touching, caressing their trunk, and talking to them, is a pure joy that is often accompanied with the reception of messages and sometimes healing from their unconditional loving nature.

I appeal to all of you who may have not yet dared to hug or touch a tree with pure love to try it. There is no shame to be in touch with Nature. Being out of touch would be to take for granted the respect that they give and show us. Trees do not judge. They only know how to love. You have to have the awareness and respect for Nature, for your planet, take the time to honor the soil you walk on, the trees that give you oxygen to breathe, the clouds that give you shade and rain, the sun that gives you warmth, nutrients and vitamins, the moss in the tropical forest, and the fairies and other beings of love that live in the absolute beauty of these magnificent places/alters on earth.

I invite you to do the following exercise the next time you are in the presence of trees. Choose a tree that is at least three times larger than your waist size. Before anything else, ask the chosen tree if it is okay to communicate with it, ask permission. If you receive a feeling that is a 'no', choose another tree without holding any judgment. If it's a yes, touch it gently, caress its leaves, its trunk, then you may hug him very gently as you enter his aura/energy field, and start conversing with him as if he were a human being. Look around and embrace any other tree, any plant, any flower, any mineral, any crystal or rock within your sight, with respect, and gratitude. Remember that anything you send out, you receive back. When you send out disrespect towards anything related to Nature or anyone, do not feel like a poor victim, or be surprised, when people begin treating you with the same disrespect later. This world does not know judgments. It only knows to give you back more of what you have given away. You are being replenished with exactly the same ingredient. Give love, and love will be given back. If you give hate, guess what you get back? I am not the creator of that logic: The Universe is!

How many of you have felt their privacy violated when someone that you are talking with comes a little bit too close to you? In response, you step backwards a little as your intuition tells you to do so, and that person makes two steps forward again. How many of you have experienced this? Was it comfortable? It is the very same impact on trees or any elements of nature as they have an aura like yours. We can start creating a better world by learning to be respectful towards each other and when I say each other, I mean each living being coexisting on this planet earth. Treat them the way you like to be treated. Also have you ever taken the time to imagine how it must feel to be a tree that is savagely killed, or taken away to another place, far from your friends? Would you ever like to have that done to you, the way we abduct animals for our selfish pleasure, and what we regularly to other elements of nature? Does anybody take the time to feel and listen to their pain? Does anybody care? Do the people that destroy them believe that this is okay just because they appear as objects rather than living beings? Does anybody feel with their heart?

Back to the exercise, now turn yourself and place your ankles, spine, neck, and back of your head against the body tree. Close your eyes and meditate, breathe in and out, send your love and receive love in return. Feel the energy of the silence. Feel the moment. Feel the tree's heartbeat, and listen to what it is telling you and/or your body, let your soul communicate with that of the tree.

Each time I go to visit them, I noticed that as soon as I have sight of the trees, and they have sight of me, they alert their tribe of my presence, and also the fairies who live there. When I bring people along during private spiritual tours, I noticed that the tree that is in connection with the person next to me will alert the others in the Cathedral of our arrival, and they start rejoicing. It is an incredibly overwhelming feeling when the elements of nature honor your presence like a King, in response to your humble acknowledgment and respect for them. Sometimes the fairies will show themselves to the people that are with me, if they feel their love and respect. They even let them take photographs. Very often, what is not visible to the eye is visible through the eye of the camera, which is very interesting. It is always a very moving, heartfelt and fulfilling experience.

I gave the example of the oasis however you are assured to find a Natural Altar in any forest or National Park. Whether it is in Yellowstone National Park, Joshua Tree National Park, Sequoia National Park, the rainforests of the Olympic National Park or in any other place where nature has remained mostly untouched, there are fairies waiting to play along with you. A good way to see them is to mentally call them forth, like you would call forth your Angels, while walking on the trails of the place you are visiting, and they will appear. Will you be aware enough to see them? Once you start seeing them, you may be surprised at how many there are.

The virtual Altar:
No matter where you are, you can co-create a virtual altar by visualizing it in your thoughts. It cannot be repeated enough, that thoughts create the beliefs that lead to its physical manifestation. You can be in a motel room in the middle of no man's land, and visualize an altar in your thoughts, feel it, meditate, pray. It can be that simple.

You are the creator of your own reality!

This is why it is improper to judge anyone, or to impose your beliefs onto someone else. Our Society does that every day of our lives, however since you are the creator of your own reality, no one can judge your own truth as it is exclusively yours!

When I was 3 years old, my altar was a wooden chicken toy that I pushed with a stick attached to it. He was with me all the time, comforting me, making me feel good, he was my friend and I loved to have him in my bed while I was sleeping. He was my very first altar, a place to recharge with good thoughts.

When I grew up, the piano and music became my altar, a place to share my thoughts and feelings, a place to heal my sadness and clear my negative thoughts. It was in this place that I was able to release the negatives to create something positive.

Several years ago, I was at a spiritual conference in Seal Beach, California where they had created a beautiful altar. The centerpiece was a statue of an Angel looking like the Virgin Mary painted with gold wings and a blue dress sparkled with scintillating golden glitter. During the intermission, there was a raffle and they announced that this centerpiece was the big prize. Everybody was craving for that statue. Some even said "Oh it's mine because I know exactly where I will put it." Everybody was already considering her as theirs, which made me look at the Virgin Mary-Angel statue. Suddenly I saw a white flash on her face which made me look twice. She wanted my attention and told me "Please buy one ticket as I want to go with you and be in your home." I stood up without hesitation and waited in the line that had formed to purchase a ticket. Actually I got 5. The raffle started with smaller items and I won 3. When the number for the big prize was spoken, I could not believe my eyes as I had the number, and I won it with the very first ticket I had bought out of the 5. If I had only bought one, like she had told me, she would have still gone home with me. She is now part of my Altar and actually part of my spiritual work. She even gets involved sometimes during private sessions.

I attempted to write this book in my office, but the inspiration was not coming along so I brought all my computer equipment into the living room area, which is surrounded by light and nice views of the San Jacinto Mountains, the palm trees, and pool, etc.

In front of the desk are my two dear friends, Archangel Gabriel on the left, and the statue of the Virgin Mary in her blue dress with golden Angel wings on the right.

Archangel Gabriel was in a store in Palm Springs. After first seeing him, my friend and I had the feeling at the same time that he wanted to go with us, and more specifically to be in my home. I listened right away. When I receive a message or a strong intuition, definite absolute impulse, I honor the request without questioning. Since then, Gabriel contributes to my reading and spiritual work too, during private sessions. Both of them are part of my life and have held the light for inspiration in the writing of this book.

Nine years ago, I learned about the crystal beds when I was living in Los Angeles, CA. I was dreaming of having one as part of my altar someday, but they were quite pricey. The bed is made of several large pieces of crystals; each carefully placed for each chakra and is covered with the natural blue colored Angelite stones. Angelite is a special healing rock that is found in the high desert of Peru. My limitations for not owning one, was based on the fear of not having sufficient financial energy (money) to pay for it. One morning, I heard the Angels say with a firm tone to get the phone, and buy that table now. I had seen it in one of my trip to a spiritual conference in Mount Shasta a few months before. A person answered and told me: "Great, I will deliver it tomorrow." I had no clue how I was going to pay for it. However I knew that every time the Angels were asking me to do something, and with a very distinct manner, the outcome would be rewarding. At the time of delivery she accepted my offer to pay with 6 different checks to be cashed one at a time for the next six months. However the Angels must have smiled when I suddenly received many calls for private sessions, and sold so many CDs during that week that I was able to pay off the crystal bed in two and a half weeks. Another miracle!

When you hear that very distinct voice from the Angels, an inner voice that urges you to do something in the now, or go somewhere immediately, you cannot oppose it, because it is so firm, direct, and precise, that you just know you have to do it. When you receive such a message, honor it without questioning. If you dare to question it, and let your brain go into motion, you will never do it and you would have missed something great. This crystal bed is now part of my altar. When I lie on it, I feel recharged. I remember a friend of mine who did not believe in such power of crystals. One day, he got extremely tired and asked me if lying on that bed could do any good for him. I told him to try it and find out for himself. He was only on the crystal bed for about 15 minutes and he got up energized like a young puppy. "It worked, it worked, it worked!" He was shouting at me, as if he needed to convince me of what I already knew. Crystals are great and many people use them for their healing purposes. I am happy to share a figure of the altar I used for the creation of this book:

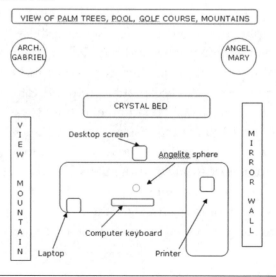

CHAPTER TWENTY

THE ANGEL ON THE MOUNTAIN & DOLPHINS IN THE SAND

As mentioned in Chapter Nine, I believe the Angel on the Mountain has guided me to relocate to the Palm Springs area in the Coachella Valley, which interpreted in the Native American language means 'The Palm of God's Hand'. This Angel can be seen from miles around, from Sky Valley to North Palm Springs, CA. However those who can see it daily from their homes are the residents of the city of Desert Hot Springs, CA, world-renowned for the best mineral waters and natural hot springs. When I lived there she brought me so much peace and comfort just by looking at her. She protects anyone that sees her with an amazing and embracing pure love.

I mentioned the 'Cathedral of Palm Trees' in a previous chapter. To me, there is a vortex at that location, and is probably due also to the San Andreas Fault. Since I moved here, I have always been intrigued by connecting the dots between the vortexes of the area. One day I finally took a detailed map and aligned the points between the Angel, the Dove and the Cathedral of Palm Trees, and my surprise was immensurable when it resulted in forming a pyramid. When you look at the great pyramid of Giza, in Egypt, you can find the King's Chamber at a very specific location within the pyramid, a location of power. When I compared the one in the desert to the one of Giza, I noticed that the King's Chamber appeared to be at the Palm Drive exit, on the Interstate 10, just near the location of my last car accident, where I believe the Angel statue sacrificed itself for me, and also where the Angel and the Christ images can be seen etched into the rock on the San Jacinto mountain. Is it just a coincidence? Palm Springs used to be called 'Agua Caliente' in the 1800s. Caliente, also being the small town near Tehachapi, CA, where the child appeared upside down in the blue sky while taking a photo of the mountain, which gave me the signs to relocate to Palm Springs. Could it be a connection between Caliente and 'Agua Caliente'? Are those just coincidences or a discovery in the making?

I feel the Angel on the mountain is a female. A story says that sometimes near the end of the nineteenth century, a railroad worker saw the Angel from afar, and asked the crew to stop for the night until this stop became a ritual. Was this Angel already there when the Cahuilla tribes lived here for over a thousand years before the invasion of the white man? What is her purpose to be here? Is it to protect us? Why is she so clearly visible for miles around? So many questions remain unanswered to this day. We know however that as everything happens for a reason,

Mother Nature did not create this phenomenon of the Angel and the Christ without a specific purpose. In my opinion, it is obviously and precisely noticeable for mankind to see.

She majestically overlooks the entrance of the Coachella Valley, naturally etched into the rock, with a significantly whiter tone than the rest of the entire mountain, which distinguishes her even more. It looks as if someone had sculpted it and then painted it in a lighter color than the mountain itself so his artwork would be seen by everyone. Most importantly, it reminds me of the Virgin Mary-Angel in my home and that I had won years ago. Each time I visit her, either alone or with people that I bring during my private tours, she always delivers positive messages just as a loving mother would do with her child. Talk to her and listen to the messages she has for you. She radiantly stands there like a beacon of Light overlooking the ocean to protect its mainland inhabitants from any danger.

I received several messages that I attempted in vain to communicate to the local media. The messages are simple. She says she is clearly exposed for anyone to be able to acknowledge her Presence. The reason she described to me in January 2009 was that in the event a sudden change due to climate, earthquake, tsunami, etc, the Angel would fade three days prior to a major event, like the fading lines of the palm of a hand of an elderly person being ready to pass away from a natural death. She is here to protect people. She also said that she made herself noticeable enough for people to be used to seeing her, so they will know something is about to occur when she significantly fades away. She also added that the fading would be considerable, as if she were to suddenly disappear. I realize that most people do not take the time to look around, being too busy with their life, and therefore even though she is so noticeable, I know of so many who drive right in front of her and even sometimes stop to take pictures of the mountain without noticing their Angel reigning above them. How blind and self absorbed do we have to be? It really makes you think that many things may actually occur right in plain site that we never pay attention to see.

The image of the Christ, an identical phenomenon as the Angel, appeared to me while composing my album, Symphony of Light, during the time when I was still living in Desert Hot Springs. His right profile looks in the same direction as the Angel, towards the east of the Valley. When I bring people to see them during private tours that I conduct, they learn how to open their hearts in order to communicate and receive messages from them. For each person it is a moving, comforting and an exhilarating experience. A lot of people feel drawn to relocate here. Could this attraction come from the Presence of the Angel, even though they are unconscious of it?

This leads me to talk about the vortexes that I have visited in the area. In most cases, they are located in the most surprising and unexpected places, sometimes in the middle of nowhere which would make you think no-one would be able to find them. The reason why people find these places is because of their powerful magnetic attraction. People know without really knowing that the place recharges their corporal batteries and what you do with that extra energy only depends upon you and your intentions. The same thing applies for the city of Desert Hot Springs, CA that receives a great source of high energy directly from the major vortex corridor, at the entrance of the Valley combined with the high velocity winds pushing that energy right thru the city plus the vortex found at the Palm Drive exit give plenty of reasons why the city overflows with tons of energy. The entrance of the valley, from Banning to Desert Hot Springs is a portal, a vortex high in energy and I have taken many pictures demonstrating this extraordinary phenomenon. I invite you to see them on my website at: *www.FredericDelarue.com/gallery.html,* then click on *'Eyes of Your Heart photographs'*.

A few hours from Palm Springs resides one of my favorite destinations; a large sand dune stretching approximately 6 miles wide by 45 miles long. This is where, like I told you earlier, I am able to see the reflection of myself, probably in a past life in the Middle East, walking towards me and dressed with a white cotton long robe and a cloth headpiece. This is where the inspiration for my album, Reflection, arose.

"Leaving my footprints on the sand dunes
is like walking on what used to be the bottom of the ocean
and I can sense the whales and dolphins energy
that once lived in this magnificent place"

It is an incredible sensation to walk these sand dunes with the awareness of their presence. I wish to share a story with you that happened while visiting this place with someone during a private tour. Not everyone will understand it but I ask you to read it with openness of spirit.

We started to walk on the dunes, heading to the specific location where I used to feel the dolphins passing thru. Suddenly I felt the presence of whales and it did not feel welcoming. The lady who was with me preferred to stay on a dune that seemed like a safe island, between the passages of the whales on the south and the dolphins on the north side of that dune. I approached the edge of the dune where the whales were and I felt terribly dizzy. The whales were not too happy of our sudden presence and wished I had announced our arrival to them before entering the dunes. I felt silly for the ignorance that the dunes may be the territory of other beings, spiritual and living, and that I had to ask permission to walk on the dune or at least to announce myself before entering their territory. After a while, they were okay with me, and told me to be careful. I joined the lady I was with, and we headed north to the location where I knew the dolphins were. Suddenly we overlooked a large basin with a pod of thousands of baby dolphins swimming and I then understood why the whales were so protective and had asked me to be careful. No one else except us, were on the dunes that day, and the special moment to feel their energy was priceless. We thought we had seen everything when my eyes perceived the mother dolphin, lying at the left edge of this great basin, to protect them. I took pictures of this moment that I also highly invite you to view on my website, as mentioned above.

There are many mysterious enigmas in this desert, between the Angel, the Christ, the Dove, the Cathedral of Palm Trees, the sand dunes in and around Palm Springs, California, a mountain in Arizona appearing to be of crystal nature, and the 'White Dove of the Desert' near Tucson, Arizona.

I took the time to align the dots of all these places on a map, which formed a long lozenge with a U.S. military base directly in the center point and I leave it up to you to feel and see through the eyes of your heart to make your own conclusions.

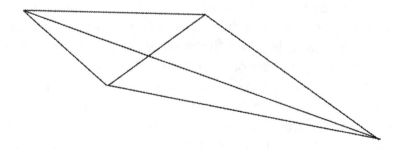

CHAPTER TWENTY ONE

Connect To Your Healing Angels

The Angels have always watched over us, as their mission is to help us to achieve our life's purpose, the one chosen by our soul, with the collaboration of the Angels, before living this current lifetime on earth. Once we have chosen the mission with the Angels, we are born on earth. The Angels watch over us throughout our entire life. It sounds simple, however many of us have forgotten their existence. That will not stop the Angels from taking action to save us in case of an emergency, such as a traffic accident when it is not yet our time to go. Most importantly, the Angels have always sent us signs to catch our attention because they know that when we open the eyes of our heart to acknowledge, see and feel them, we will never feel alone or lonely again. They want us to feel comforted by their presence and their unconditional love.

The Healing Angels:

We live a soul's life as a human experience, which combines the soul, the mind, and the body. Creating a balance between these three things is what keeps us centered, healthy and happy. When one of them becomes unbalanced, the Angels will try to catch your attention. If you miss their warning signs, your body then attempts to gently to tell you that something is out of control and needs to be regulated by manifesting a physical reaction or dis-ease. The ego often has its share of responsibility in this. When you choose to live your life though the mastermind of the ego, this little entity rapidly becomes you, what you think, and what you want. This causes you to progressively disconnect you from your true Self and eventually leads into the early stage of dis-ease and dis-function, manifesting illness within the body as a result of your imbalance. The symptoms may begin gradually, such as light headaches, or a small tummy ache, etc., and progressively worsens with stronger corporal discomfort. If you still choose to not listen to any of these subtle warning signs, the body will be forced to perform with more intensity, in an attempt to catch your attention, to say "hello, do you hear me?" It is a little bit like a radio, and the messages are received by the antenna of your Higher Source. When the volume is too low, you need to turn it up a little more in order to hear the message properly. It can go on like that for years until one day a big co-created earthquake will manifest a major 'virtual' illness. I like to use the term 'virtual' here because although the illness is indeed felt within the body and doctors may agree it is physically and realistically there, however, from a spiritual perspective and point of view, if you choose to believe that the body cannot be sick (with the affirmation that as God created you as his image, he cannot have created a sick body), this illness becomes a virtual temporary disease that will stay with you until you have done your spiritual work, by giving total forgiveness, or totally surrendering and accept fully to allow the 'old you' to die by releasing its old patterns and ties, to give birth to a 'new you' totally healthy and balanced (later explained in this chapter).

When one learns about the appearance of a disease, we often will not see it as the only way the body has found to get your attention to get back on track, because the ego refuses to face its own responsibility, therefore the blame is directed towards anything or anyone else, sometimes even God, and the disease is then perceived as a sad fatality. We may eventually fight it, fight it, and fight it again, instead of trying to understand the core essence of why it came to disturb a body that has been created to be healthy. When you fight something that is within the body, the Angels always warn us of the consequences. With each battle, a winner and a loser will emerge. Some will win, using the power of their minds, others with the power of surrendering, and others will lose when they accept the fatality.

When you have the courage to believe that you are the co-creator of the destiny of your own life, you can quickly understand that you have then the power of overcome anything. The Angels of God are always there to help us to surrender to accomplish this. The body's discomfort is only the reflection of the imbalance of your soul, the mirror that reflects to you that something is out of control in your life. The pain exists only to serve as a WARNING ALERT to your awareness, and not to hurt or harm you.

Example: If you put your finger too close to a flame, it will hurt. The body is letting you know that it hurt, so you know that you need to quickly remove your finger from the flame. Substitute the flame to any area in your life that is bringing you, or may have brought you in the past, unhappiness, discomfort, sadness, or any other trauma.

The reason I took the time to talk about the ego in this chapter of the Healing Angels is just because of its irony. The Angels are here to help us live a happy and healthy life, whereas most of us choose to let their pride and their ego handle any situation they encounter, which brings forth dis-ease. Will you decide to surrender and call forth the Angels? It is a choice that we all have to make and be responsible for. Again, I wish to make it clear that this is the Angels' messages that I am transmitting to you. I am only the vessel of their inspired words of wisdom. Like in everything else, God gave you the free will to do whatever you wish to do with any type of information, so you may decide to fully accept, or deny and refuse them. Nothing is ever imposed upon you as you have always the choice to tell your mind and your body what you want to believe. Think of that.

All subjects in relation to the ego and the power we give to it become controversial, as it touches the sensitive aspect of living a life governed by your true Self, the one connected to the Divine Source, or a life mostly filled with illusionary moments, ideas, and concepts. Are you living a life that is not totally yours with the illusion that it is, or are you already living your true life? Those are the questions you want to ask yourself, which can help you considerably to grow spiritually.

I like to think of a disease, an illness, or an accident, as an opportunity for us to get back on track to our chosen path. It all comes down to this; as a soul, we choose a mission to accomplish, or a lesson to go through, or to be an earthly angel to help a dear long time soul friend in his/her mission, etc. When we get away from that mission, the Angels of God and our body (the lifetime home that is needed to achieve that mission on this physical earth) will attempt to let us know of the distraction that has occurred, and when we do not listen to any of these signs, the body will create something bigger to force us to see. If that still doesn't get our attention, God will create something even bigger, like he created for me, becoming paralyzed from the waist down, in the only attempt for me to see, and forgive myself for not following my life purpose, and then totally surrender. When I give my power to the ego or to anyone that has provoked anger in me, I lose my power and the strength of clarity and discernment. However when I give my power to God, or to the Angels, I receive my strength back as I align my true self to the pure divine Creation.

Using the experiences of my life that I detailed in previous chapters, these 'bad events' in the form of accidents and being paralyzed were not disasters nor tragedies, but blessings in disguise because I chose to see positively, what I had to learn from each of these events. It takes a great unconditional Faith to do so, and then comes another opportunity for all of us to think of our own Faith. I do not love or hate God depending on the illusionary appearances of the events occurring in my life. I know there is a higher reason behind every event and it is my only choice to see, hear, feel, and act upon it either positively or negatively. I have total Faith so I accept fully, forgive all involved, included myself and others for what could have been done better, without judgment, and surrender. Not even God is judging us, so who are we to judge others? It is once again the illusion of the ego that makes us judge so we can be right all the time, instead of evaluating ourselves and our own actions.

We have just discussed the possibility that when an illness comes in, it is usually because the body is yelling, screaming at you, only to wish that you will finally hear and surrender! Now what is your body trying to tell you? That's a good question. The body in itself is not sick. The body is made on God's image so it is perfectly balanced with every single ingredient to regulate itself in case of small imbalances. The body is only trying to exteriorize all the pain and trauma that you were unable to face, vocalize or forgive unconditionally. When you face a physical issue, you want to ask yourself "What did I not succeed to exteriorize so my body had to do it for me?" Your body does not declare war on itself. It only attempts to help you, by bringing awareness through this imbalance, so you can start surrendering by giving away your pain to the Angels of God, by forgiving yourself for not listening sooner and also by forgiving whoever co-created this trauma or whatever caused it. Forgiveness is essential. Blaming only contributes to the continuity of the pain to others. Incest is a typical trauma that, when not stopped, healed or forgiven, perpetuates from generation to generation. Do you wish to be responsible and create something good in your life? Forgive! When someone has hurt you, blaming that person only creates more turbulence, hateful thoughts and vibes within you, and without considering it, may as a chain reaction, affect your close entourage as well. What if that person just did to you what someone else did to him/her, without succeeding to forgive totally, and as a result, this unfortunate cycle of abuse has taken form towards you? By forgiving, you cut the ties, the patterns to that continuity. Ask the Angels to help you to forgive. They are here for that also.

When I chose not to listen for 17 years, giving priority to my fear that I would not find the right healer and Angel reader to help me to develop my natural intuitive gifts, fear to tell everyone about my communication with the Angels and my NDE. My body was probably yelling at me for my highest best interest. It could have declared an illness within to catch my attention and to stop me from running away from my path, but instead I was paralyzed from this medical error. I believe as well that if my reaction had given priorities to anger, blame and lawsuit, I may still be paralyzed today. But as I got it, as the message of why this incident happened was understood, it was instantly released, and only took 8 months to completely walk normally again. I had chosen the acceptance of it all, because I acknowledged in the moment my disconnection to the Source, to my true Self. I was honest and extremely sincere to myself about it.

All that I share with you is only to expand your awareness, vision and perception. It is not, in any way, to confront any medical reasoning or institution. I can only talk about my own experiences and what I know from my communication with the Angels.

After hearing the lady's testimonial about her misaligned and damaged dorsal disk being healed during a one hour and a half musical meditation that I had given at the Spiritual Enrichment Center in Palm Springs in 2002, during the time that Drs. Ernest and Florence Phillips were the Ministers, you know that anything is possible for you, too. This healing took place, because she was in full acceptance and surrender towards the situation, which helped whatever was causing this misalignment and pain to be gently rel(ease)d with ease and peace. The limitations are only what you tell your mind. If you think it is not possible, the thought creating the belief which creates the physical manifestation of the statement you co-created will give you the result that it is not possible. But if you choose to believe that anything is possible (as God has created you at his image), your mind being free from the concept of limitations, restrictions and so forth, than anything will be possible. The outcome depends on you, and how free you want and claim to be. In my own opinion, believing that one may be a sinner while also believing that we were made at God's image is a contradictory that can only bring confusion on any level of one's life.

The Angels invite us constantly to surrender. Their healing message is that it only takes one second of complete surrender for you to be blessed, wherever the area of the blessing is needed. One second! Imagine, you may have lived many years with an imbalance in your body, and one second can provoke the healing, the cure, in an instant. This is what happens with all the miracles occurring in Lourdes, France. Do they take place because of the location of Lourdes or because of people's strong beliefs they may be healed at that location? Actually it may be a little bit of both, having personally experienced the resonance of the grotto. Whether you touch the grotto or let the power of soothing music resonate and radiate through you, it all comes from succeeding to abandon yourself, with all of your pain and misery, to the power of God (your Higher Source), for only one second to see your blessings manifested.

This is the teaching of Jesus when He brought me to the top of the hill and asked me to watch Him do His healings. People were surrendering totally thanks to the power of the high energetic vibration of His aura. But like Jesus told me, this is what also occurs when you surrender totally through the power of the angelic soothing music. Anywhere you can find yourself to surrender totally, whether or not you use tools (music, meditation, spiritual group, in nature or through visualization), please do it for your highest and best interest to bring forth healing and balance into your life.

A suggested way to surrender is when you can actually say and sincerely feel with your heart, the following:

"I kneel, let go and abandon unconditionally
my power to God, to the Higher Source of my Self.
My old Self accepts to die now,
with the powerful abundance of peace and forgiveness,
to be reborn strong and healthy and totally free."

When you are able to say this with a true sincerity in your heart and soul, and when you feel that dark energy, whatever it may be, being released from your solar plexus, into the ether, to be divinely purified, you know the old you has died, and allowed the new healthy you to be born again in one magical instant.

Here are a few ways to connect to your Angels. Use the basic and add any specification that you wish to expand upon your request.

How to connect to your Angels (basic connection):
Stand or sit straight and while bringing your hands towards the sky, (at the level of your shoulders if that's possible), take a deep belly breath and let the thoughts of your mind go; exhale from the mouth; take a second deep belly breath and feel your body getting relaxed; exhale from the mouth; take a third deep belly breath and empty your mind totally, and exhale from the mouth. Be in the silence and the stillness of who you truly are. Recall the beautiful Soul that you are and remain still. Feel the peace invading your entire body. Call the Angels forth with an intention. Knowing their names are not necessary as the ones available at that moment, for the needed purpose and mission will come to you. Feel the Angels' Love enveloping your entire body. Acknowledge and appreciate each second, with utmost gratitude.

(Choose your specific prayer to them – see below)

Thank them and be grateful for their presence and their unconditional loving help. Be also thankful to yourself, say 'I love myself' to yourself while taking time to feel it, and start opening your eyes slowly. Be fully conscious of your body.

CHAPTER TWENTY ONE

Wish:

Ask your Angels your wish: Basic connection +Tell them your highest wish(es) with a clear and most precise description and feel it released into the ether. You have given that wish to them. Be relaxed until total peace and calmness has penetrated every part of you.

Healing/Cure:

Ask your Angels for a healing or cure: Basic connection + Express to them the physical painful manifestation in your body and ask them to help you to accept it gracefully (as you know there may be a reason for it to have come knocking on your door – in your body) and feel humble enough to surrender, to abandon yourself, your pain, and the cause of the pain, to them. Kneel if it helps you to surrender, to let go of all, to allow the old you to die with its illness, to see the new you be reborn. Breathe gently and bathe in the stillness of the silence of the new you and power that you are getting back. Be grateful and thankful.

Decision:

How to ask your Angels to help you make a decision: Whether you want to ask for a situation, a job or a person, such as a friend or a potential sentimental partner, we will name it 'A'.

Start with the basic connection + Tell the Angels "If 'A' is good for my highest and best interest, please show me a sign; if 'A' is not good for me, show me a sign and reject it from me." It has the charm to be very short but beware, very sharp. When the question is asked firmly and precisely and with the most sincerity, the answer will come back to you the same way. For example, if A is good for you and it was regarding a person, that person might in the next twenty four hours do something nice but unusual such as calling you and say the nicest things to you, or giving you a surprising nice present. If on the contrary, that person creates an argument, bad words are exchanged, or if the person unusually disappears for the next two days when prior to that you were having news from that person, you will know that your answer is it is not in your highest best interest.

The Angels numbers: 11:11; 1:11; 4; 4:44, etc:

Often the Angels aim to use the numbers above to grasp your attention, as a wake up call. Why do they appear to you? Have you ever watched the clock and see 11:11 repeatedly in the course of your life or during a determined period of time. What was your main preoccupation of thoughts at that time the numbers appeared to you? Perhaps the Angels just wanted to let you know that they are with you, and that all is going to be fine?

Also, like your body tries to get your attention when something is unbalanced in your life, the Angels try to catch your attention with numbers for the same purpose. Seeing the same numbers all the time should excite your curiosity and that's what they are hoping for. They wish you to start wondering what it means and start talking about it. Eventually that will bring you to find someone that knows, to view a website about it or to read this book, for instance. Often the fact to see these numbers is to comfort you with a validation in relation to your main thoughts of the moment. Angels do not like to see us worried therefore they invented the 'Angel Code' as a validation. I am certain they are validating my book in its entirety if I consider all the time I have seen 11:11, 1:11 in each day and night. One night they woke me up with a message for the introduction page of this book. At first, I did not want to wake up, but learning from the experiences of the past when I had missed the divine information given to me, I woke up, turned on the light and it was 4:11 am. When you see these types of numbers, you know it is them talking to you. That's just the way they are.

With some practice, you may even hear them laugh out loud. They are good teasers and very playful too but the Angels also share their frustration to see people struggling when they could have helped them, however they cannot help someone if they have not been called upon. Only in some cases of emergency, such as during accidents, etc, may they intervene without permission if this is, in fact, not 'your time' to go. In other words, they watch over us, but cannot intrude unless for an unexpected occurrence demanding immediate action.

What do they look like?

Again, it depends on which ones you are talking about. There is a hierarchy of Archangels and Angels. The ones I have encountered the most are very tall, taller than a regular height of a house, between 8 to 20 feet tall and between 3 to 6 feet wide. If you deal with Cherubs, of course they are much smaller.

Do human Angels exist?

Yes definitely. Angels may appear under human forms. Many who have had a NDE narrate they, as a soul, could fly through walls. Of course, at a soul level, physical matter is not an obstacle anymore. Angels have of course this ability as well. Perhaps you even have a close friend, whose mission was to watch over you!? It reminds me of a story I had heard a long time ago, the one of a corporate business man in New York City whom every day while going to his office would pass near a homeless person. This business man never paid attention to this homeless man. One day, this workaholic man, who had no time for love, felt so stressed, depressive that he decided to call a friend of his with psychic abilities. Even though he was more the non believer type, out of disarray, he asked her what to do. She told him that he had to see his brother. He replied that he did not have any brother and started to think she had no gifts at all. She insisted by saying that there was his brother waiting for him, willing to love him and she added "He is so close to you that you do not see him." The conversation ended a few minutes later and he left the office like every day. He was focusing on this conversation that intrigued him a lot, and when he passed near the homeless person, a vision enveloped him. The homeless man looked at him, with tears in his eye. This man was in fact his old loving brother of another life that came in this lifetime as a homeless to teach his other brother to be more loving and generous. He was there every day in hope that his brother would think of other people, by giving him some heartfelt generosity. The business man took the homeless man into his home, made of him an honorable person, gave him a job in his company and both became very happy and successful. It may sound like a fantasy la-la land kind of Hollywood movie, but it is the story. This homeless man was actually his earthly angel. His mission was to wait in hope for the business man to wake up from his egoistic, flat and flavorless life. He succeeded to finally see his brother in the eyes of his heart.

Here is another story of a human Angel, personal this time that I would like to share with you. I told you in Chapter Twelve that during my last car accident where Jesus appeared, Charles my nephew had had angelic visions of very tall Angels with golden diamond wings healing a man lying on a hospital bed. I have also shared with you in Chapter Eight that a child had appeared with his face upside down, with very distinct eyes, to help me to relocate to the Palm Springs area, California. What I have not told you yet and that I am going to reveal now is that this child was nobody else but Charles, who was 8 at the time, who appeared 4 years ahead of his time to help me to relocate. This is why I did not recognize the boy when the event occurred. I realized that after his mom sent me new pictures of him at age 13. It was a shock looking at the astounding similarity of the two photos. He is another earthly Angel.

I meet a lot of people who seem to limit themselves asking what the names of their Angels are, so they can talk to them. Please do not limit yourself with names. It does not really matter. What matters the most is the purpose for the help requested. Is it for healing, for a job, for attention, care, for a partner, for a situation, etc.? Call them forth with that specific intention and the ones available at that time for the mission and purpose requested will come to help you.

Blindly trust their presence and always remember to thank them afterwards for any service you have solicited.

A question that I am asked often is:
How do I know the answers come from the Angels and not from my imagination?
Very simple! If the answer varies in its consistency, it comes from your imagination. The Angels will always say and repeat the same thing over and over until it is understood and completed.

Do I need anything special to meditate?
It depends on you. There is no good, bad, right or wrong recipe. Some like to have a ritual with incense, music of your choice, candles, etc whereas others can meditate anywhere in an impetus of spontaneity, such as meditating in a forest, at the beach, at sunset, sunrise, anywhere in the house, watching clouds, observing Nature and its insects, animals, fairies, etc. However what you need is time, time to unleash, and to not feel rushed. A meditation can be done in one minute or one hour but it is necessary to not feel rushed as this feeling contracts the muscles of the body that send the information to the brain, which blocks any possible direct channeling. Meditating for a longer periods of time obviously does not make it better than a short meditation. A very distinct meditation of only one minute can be just

as powerful. There are no rules and therefore no limitations either. Just be available to give and receive, to be receptive to the messages that may come through for your benefit. Be attentive at 360°. Expecting an answer from only one point of view, from one angle of the room, from one aspect of your understanding or knowledge, may cause you to miss the answer. Be open to any type of revelation.

How can I develop intuition?

Intuition is something that we all have naturally, however in a Society that assists us too well for it to be for our best interest, that tells you what is right, wrong, good and bad, so you do not have to worry about having a discernment of your own truth. Therefore many of us have forgotten the power that we have within, power of discernment, power of clarity, power of perceptibility, the power to manifest. With practice, your intuition will come back as you learn to develop it. An easy way to develop your intuition is to sit comfortably from your home and fixate on a tree in the distance, for example. Focus the eyes on that distinct tree till the object becomes kind of blurry and watch what is around the tree. Can you see its aura, the energy emanating from that tree? You can also be outside and look at the blue sky and after some time of concentrating on it, see if you can see a transparent energy moving. With practice, you can do this with yourself: watch yourself from above (as if you were the eyes of a camera on top of a corner of the room), then once you see it clearly, expand that vision by moving that camera higher in the sky, and so forth, until you can have a wide, global vision of your life, of a situation, and clarity on the options that we may have, that you could not see from a down-to-earth perspective.

Another very easy way is to ask a friend to help do the following: Have three empty cubes, or something similar to tea/coffee cups. Ask your friend to place a key or any object of your choice under one the cups. All you will see is three cups turned upside down. Place your hands on each cup while focusing on the energy of the key or whatever the object may be and pick one cup. See if you found it. Another way is focalizing on each cup and to try to see/feel the object through the object through the cups. And finally, another way is to use your instinct. See which ones you are best at, and that will give you an idea of the stage of your perception. In the event you haven't yet succeeded to find the hidden item, persist to practice without forcing or feeling any frustration. Like in anything, expecting too much, or forcing to receive will only block the blessing from reaching you. Practice calmly, with serenity and enjoy the process.

I see so many people telling me that they keep asking the Angels for help but they never receive any answers. They feel alone and not loved from the Angels.

First, it has to be accepted, once for all, that the Angels love every one of you. They do not have the ability to judge nor to punish. Their nature is to love and help unconditionally when solicited. It is common to our co-creation, thinking we are endless wrongdoers. This is not part of the Angelic World of God. To feel unworthy of it all because of an illusionary sin has no sense in their language. Again let me repeat that if you believe in sin, you cannot also believe that you have been created at God's image. It is totally contradictory. The Angels working for God are made of pure Love. Now you must decide for yourself whether you think God is pure Love or not. Again, be responsible of your actions, beliefs and behaviors, but feeling one way just because you are being told to do so, is not responsible. By being submissive, you are like good sheep under the control of their shepherd. Again, ask yourself if God is pure Love or God is a control freak? Instead of focusing on the weaknesses you may have or be as a human being, focus on your strength, on all the things that you are, or can become again. Remain positive by rejecting the negative. Forget the false side of vulnerability and remember your resiliency, and the good side of vulnerability that is to abandon and surrender yourself to the strength of your Higher Source.

The Angels will respond to your request when:

1) They are solicited.

2) They have understood the request. Don't be afraid to be very specific.

Most of the time, the question you may ask is so confusing and not structured well, that the Angels do not understand anything that you are telling them and therefore cannot give you a precise answer. Structure your question and be as clear and simple as possible. Don't expect the Angels to respond with a 360 page book. They will answer by 'yes' or by 'no' in most cases, send you messages in the instant, or you will make sense of them in the two days following your request. Remember, you receive what you send out. If you are sending out a confused and complicated question, your answer will be the same.

The Angels aspire to you taking some time for yourself each day, to find the silence within and to feel your roots, your feet touching the earth, and your soul elevated to the celestial realm of God, that is a pure Source of Love, which opens up the doors of clarity, truth and discernment within yourself.

Meditate like a strong ancient tree of wisdom. Feel the sacredness, the strength, the stillness of the tree within you, even when your life appears to be in the torment of a storm. Stay grounded and consciously feel the Divinity in the presence of every living, breathing Being on this earth; whether it is in the moss, in the rocks, in the plants, in the vegetation surrounding you at the moment being, the forest, the trees, the breeze caressing your face, the moistness in the air layering your skin, the scents of the joy felt, or any fragrance of Nature. Have this relationship with the present moment.

The Angels like to tell you not to forget to say thank you to those that you love and do not forget yourself. Take the time to embrace yourself, to place your arms around you and give yourself the Love that you deserve. If you are one of those who think that no-one else gives you love, at least give it to yourself. It's a good start to remind yourself once again that what you send out, you receive, so if you start loving yourself, being tender and respectful to yourself, you will receive it back one way or another. Make sure to remain sincere and say thank you meaningfully, coming from the heart. Saying a nice thing to someone, just to flatter the ego, will only trigger others to be false with you. When you say thank you to someone, be sure it is a sincere acknowledgment. Respect any living being as you wish to be respected.

Talking about respect, the Angels remind me to talk about the respect between adults, parents and their children. Using my own experience, I was raised in an environment where children had no right to speak. If you were not an adult, your opinion was not welcomed or taken seriously and therefore I was never asked about my feelings. Most parents would say "Come on, don't listen to him, he is just a kid. How could he know?" Have you ever heard this said to someone else or to yourself? Or have you ever said this to a child?

Very often when I perform live at street fairs, I see children being totally drawn to the music. Their eyes are looking right into mine and they feel as if they are frozen by the connection they remember. A child is connected whereas an adult often loses his connection after our education with school progresses and through the robotic rituals that our Society teaches: the famous Do's and Don'ts. So many times, these children want to stay at my booth listening to the music, while their parents shout at them and aggressively pull them away.

They will turn back till I am out of their sight. Children have more things to say probably than adults because they are still connected to the Source, to where they come from, and to their original Soul. That's why they love dolphins because they remember their connection with them in the spatiotemporal space.

I also knew an adult who had many worries and stress and did not know what to do, what decisions to make, etc. I asked her if she talked to her child about it. She looked at me as if I had said something grotesque. I explained it to her and asked her to give it a try. Her child would know spontaneously the answer of her problems because he was still connected to the global vision of the Source he had left only a few years back without being emotionally attached to the importance or the impact of the answer. She called me two days later astonished of the firmness of his answer which appeared to be extremely accurate. Parents have little psychics in their homes and they still stress running out of answers. Go figure! A child is usually a natural psychic and medium till the age of 8 or 9 years old. Have you never heard a child tell you that she spoke with Grandma that came to visit her in her dream at night? Or have you ever heard your child say that she was just speaking with Grandpa while apparently she was alone in the room? Some children even receive a spanking for doing this, as parents think they are playing a foolish game. Who is the silliest? Always the ones that are disconnected will judge the connected ones!

The Angels also would like to say something about tithing or giving to your Spiritual Source of Inspiration and Motivation. When you go to church, and you excuse yourself to go use the restroom in order to leave just before the collection plate is passed around, or give only a few coins when that is less than you can afford to give, once again, think back of the universal law of attraction. You would not want to cheat yourself, would you? Always give to others the best you would have given to yourself.

We can co-create our Heaven on earth just as well as we can co-create our own living Hell. One is the result of the openness of our awareness whereas the other is the consequence of our ignorance. It is your choice.

A good alternative:

Start living your own life
Believe in your own truth
The one that is found looking through the eyes of your heart!

CHAPTER TWENTY TWO

WHAT IF...

In this chapter, I wish that you accept the opportunity to think and feel outside of the box as a different tool to create a new life through the eyes of your heart. Often we limit ourselves to only what our physical eyes can see. Many times we hear blind people saying that since they lost their vision, they were able to see more. When you close your eyes, and focus in the power of the silence of your being, of your soul, you may be able to see and hear even more through the eyes of your heart.

After learning from my NDE when I was 12, that what I see with my physical eyes is perhaps only 10 to 15% of what is, it has always made me push the limits to become aware of what is beyond that 10 to 15% that we know. I consider the possibilities of regressing to DNA cell memory. I know that through my eyes, I can only see the surface and appearance of what is, but through the eyes of my heart, I can see the truth, the source of that appearance, and the vision of what really is. I hope that you too, will experiment and find out for yourself your own truth through the eyes of your heart.

What if the trees are not just trees?
Have you ever asked them who they are?

What if mountains are not just mountains?

What if Atlantis is not lost underneath the oceans?

What if Atlantis was right in front of you, but it had another appearance than you expected? Would you see it?

What if the biggest secrets of all time were hiding right in plain sight? Would you see them or miss them because their appearance is something so ordinary?

What if the Elohims created life on Earth?

What if UFOs are visiting us on earth?

What if some clouds are not just clouds?

What if other more advanced beings, or ancient civilizations are living underneath us or above us?

What if there are Beings living in other planets and galaxies?

What if we had more power than we thought we had?

What if mountains, rocks, minerals, plants had a voice?
What would they tell you?
Have you taken the time to talk to any of them?

What if you were not crazy to talk to a flower
that caught your attention? Could it change your life?

What if the hummingbird, roadrunner or the butterfly
that comes to visit has a message for you? Would you know it?

What if we all started remembering who we truly are?

What if we all started to see with the eyes of our hearts?

Are you willing to participate to this global awakening
that could change the entire World?

EPILOGUE

I sincerely wish that you were able to keep an open heart through the reading of this book, even if you encountered any topics that somewhat may have disturbed the comfort zone of your beliefs and made you think about the knowledge received from the source of your beliefs. Everything is based on perception and what you allow yourself to perceive from any event that will either ease or obscure your own life.

At 12 years old, I had the awareness of the existence of the Angels and Beings of Light during a Near Death Experience that opened me up to perceive my life but also life in general with a much wider and expanded global vision in the scheme of things. This is also when I became conscious of the earthly pain we co-create for ourselves from fear and learned that the detachment from my corporal body brought me an unlimited panel of possibilities of expression of movements and a total freedom.

When you accept and succeed to detach yourself from any linked negative emotions from the appearance of a tragic event, you have earned the benefits of the blessing in disguise.

Through the various experiences of our lives, we are shown that there is always a choice for us to make. The time of rejection from others because of the difference that others perceived of me during my childhood and the adolescence forced me to spend a lot of time with myself, observing the clouds, nature, my piano, my dog, and learning more about who I truly am. When I learned to exteriorize any negative thoughts being released into a creative inspired piece of music, my heart bloomed with sparkles of joy. Instead of feeling like a victim from the rejection, I chose to see the positive side of the event, what was the Godly message behind the rejection, the greater picture.

Surrendering to what life brings us, knowing that everything does happen for a reason and is guided by a Higher Source that we can call God. Other's in the situation, as when I became paralyzed from a medical error, would have certainly chosen to blame the doctors for what they would have co-created themselves by not following their path and listening to their heart, I chose to surrender to the doctors' so-called mistake, which revealed itself to be the greatest blessing in disguise as it brought me back to my path.

Follow your dreams and your life purpose! Whatever brings you an ecstasy of joy within your heart, whenever this openness of spirit makes you jump towards the ceiling from joy, this is your dream and/or your life purpose. Focus on following it, and visualize living it instead of thinking on the details of how you will do it. Blindly trust the joy felt in your heart. Blindly trusting in my Faith is what brought me from a small French village to live in Paris, then to move to Los Angeles, and currently Palm Springs, California.

Life can be like a treasure quest: one step at a time by listening to your intuition, your inner voice, and the message of the Angels.

In many situations, remember Jesus' Aura when you are to make a responsible decision. If you open your heart to the infinite pure love, like Jesus' magnificent Aura, you will bring forth healing and clarification of situations just by your presence. If you choose to hold onto anger, jealousy, etc., that will automatically be felt in your aura, and will pollute your thoughts in addition to your close entourage with negation.

Learn discernment between what your heart feels and what you have been told to believe. Be aware of the tricks that your ego may play with you, to define yourself with the soul and person that you truly are, vs. what you want or own.

Create an altar anywhere you are, at home, in your car, or in nature to center yourself with calm and positive emotions.

And last but not least, connect to the Angels. They are waiting for you to call them forth to help you in your journey.

If you ever feel bored, start looking at the beauty of nature, feel the vibrations of the elements of nature, listening to their sounds, their breaths.

Despite all the trivial problems that we may encounter in our lifetime, life is ultimately beautiful and extraordinarily generous when we look at it from a much highly spirited perspective. It is not the value of our home or anything else that we own that creates our happiness, it's what we allow our heart to see and feel. For example, the next time you see a breath taking view, appreciate the wonder and the beauty of everything that you see and create your Million Dollar moment. It is what you do with what you see and feel in every breath you take in your life that holds the greatest value. Start doing this exercise when you allow yourself to see something extraordinarily magnificent. Look around and start appreciating the priceless life you are living.

Always remember to see through the eyes of your heart what your physical eyes are unable to see.

If we all participate to perceive and visualize a world of peace and compassion through the eyes of our heart, we will all be contributing to co-recreate a new life on earth!

Just
Imagine
what your life
could be if you allowed
the true radiance of you
to enter the kingdom of your heart.
Surrender your ego to let
the eyes of your heart
be the foundation
of your new
life.

LINKS

BOOKS:

Vannier, Marie-Emilia. *L'arbre guérisseur* & *L'arbre et l'étoile*. 2002.   www.marieemiliavannier.com

Secondé, Jean-Claude. *Numerous Books on Energy and Nutrition, written in French.*   www.jcseconde.com

Polesel-Secondé, Hélène. *A l'écoute des Anges.* Fernand Lanore Editions, 1999.   www.helenemedium.com

Delarue, Frédéric. *Eyes of Your Heart.*   Frederic Delarue Productions, 2009.   www.FredericDelarue.com

MUSIC CDs:

Compilation Album: *Cousteau's Dream*. Real Music. 2000.
www.realmusic.com

Frederic Delarue Productions' music:

Voyage of the Soul	2001
Soaring with the Angels	2003
Dolphins… A Message of Love	2004
Symphony of Light	2006
Reflection	2007
A Mind like an Ocean	2007
Eyes of Your Heart	2009

www.FredericDelarue.com

ART:

Sakmar-Sullivan, Eva. '*A Mind Like An Ocean*'. 2007
Original Artwork for the album of the same name
www.stardolphin.com

ORDERING INFORMATION

BOOK & MUSIC CD: *"Eyes of Your Heart"*

 Order Online:

Visit my website at: **www.FredericDelarue.com**

 Order by Phone:

Call toll-free (U.S. & Canada only) at 1-800-863-1885

VISA, Mastercard, Discover and Amex are accepted.

 Order by Mail:

Book: $16.95 + $3.50 postage (USA & Canada)
Music CD: $16.99 + $2.00 postage (USA & Canada)
Book + Music CD: $30.00 + $5.80 postage (USA & Canada)

(CA residents add 8.75% sales tax)

Send the amount of the items ordered in U.S. funds, plus postage to:

Frederic Delarue Productions
P.O. Box 799
Palm Springs, CA 92263-0799

Additional Postage:

Add $ 3.00 per purchase by Priority Mail (U.S. & Canada)
Add $10.00 per purchase (Europe, Asia, Australia, Africa)

Orders are usually processed within 24 hours.
Sales Tax and Postage rates are subject to change.

To write Frédéric:

Frederic Delarue Productions
P.O. Box 799
Palm Springs, CA 92263-0799

Please enclose a self-addressed stamped envelope for reply.

For more information, please visit my website at:
www.FredericDelarue.com

INDEX PAGES

PERSONAL NOTES

PERSONAL NOTES

PERSONAL NOTES